NICARAG
TRAVEL GUIDE

2024 Edition

Unveiling The Hidden Gems Of Central America's Jewel, Discover It's Breathtaking Landscapes, Vibrant Culture, And The Rich History Of Nicaragua.

Jim Baxter

TABLE OF CONTENT

Important Notice Before You continue Reading

Step into the pages of this travel guide and prepare for a truly extraordinary experience. Delve into the captivating world of Nicaragua, where imagination, creativity, and a thirst for adventure reign supreme. You won't find any images within these pages, as we firmly believe in the power of firsthand exploration, devoid of visual filters or preconceptions. Each monument, every nook and cranny eagerly awaits your arrival, ready to astonish and amaze. Why spoil the thrill of that initial glimpse, that overwhelming sense of wonder? So get ready to embark on an unparalleled journey, where your imagination becomes the sole means of transportation and you, the ultimate guide. Release any preconceived notions and allow yourself to be transported to an authentic Nicaragua brimming with hidden treasures. Let the enchantment commence, but remember, the most breathtaking images will be the ones painted by your own eyes.

Unlike many conventional guides, this book needs no detailed maps. Why, you may ask? Because we firmly believe that the truest discoveries happen when you wander, when you surrender to the current of the surroundings and embrace the uncertainty of the path. No rigid itineraries or precise directions are provided here, for we yearn for you to explore Nicaragua on your own terms, unbound by limitations or restrictions. Surrender yourself to the currents and unearth hidden gems that no map could reveal. Be audacious, follow your instincts, and brace yourself for serendipitous encounters. The magic of the journey commences now, within a world without maps, where roads materialize with each step and the most extraordinary adventures await in the folds of the unknown.

Introduction

Welcome to the enchanting land of Nicaragua, a country brimming with natural wonders, vibrant culture, and a rich history. Nestled in the heart of Central America, Nicaragua beckons travelers with its irresistible allure. As you step foot into this captivating destination, you will find yourself immersed in a world of stunning landscapes, warm-hearted people, and a tapestry of experiences that will leave you in awe.

Nicaragua is often referred to as the "land of lakes and volcanoes," and for good reason. The country is home to an impressive number of lakes, including the expansive Lake Nicaragua, the largest lake in Central America. These glistening bodies of water, framed by picturesque shores, offer a serene and tranquil escape. Moreover, Nicaragua boasts an extraordinary number of volcanoes, both dormant and active, which punctuate its landscapes with their majestic presence. The towering peaks, such as the iconic Momotombo and the mystical Masaya Volcano, add a touch of mystique to the country's natural beauty.

Beyond the lakes and volcanoes, Nicaragua is adorned with pristine beaches that stretch along its Pacific coastline. From the popular surf spots of San Juan del Sur to the secluded coves of the Corn Islands in the Caribbean Sea, there is a beach for every taste. Whether you're seeking the thrill of catching the perfect wave or simply longing for peaceful relaxation on soft golden sands, Nicaragua's beaches will surpass your expectations.

Venture further inland, and you'll find yourself ensconced in lush rainforests that brim with biodiversity. These tropical jungles are teeming with an array of flora and fauna, providing a haven for nature lovers and wildlife enthusiasts. Embark on a trek through the dense foliage, and you may encounter howler monkeys swinging through the treetops, colorful toucans perched on branches, and elusive jaguars prowling in their natural habitats. The sheer abundance of life in Nicaragua's rainforests is nothing short of extraordinary.

As you delve into Nicaragua's history, you'll discover a tapestry of civilizations and events that have shaped the nation. From the ancient indigenous cultures that once thrived in the region to the arrival of Spanish conquistadors and the subsequent colonial period, the country's history is etched in its architecture, traditions, and local customs. The cities of Granada and León stand as testaments to Nicaragua's colonial past, with their meticulously preserved Spanish colonial buildings, cobblestone streets, and vibrant plazas. Exploring these historic cities will transport you back in time, allowing you to witness the legacy of a bygone era.

Prepare to be enchanted by the symphony of natural wonders, immersed in the vibrancy of the local culture, and enthralled by the tales of a rich and diverse history. Nicaragua beckons you to embark on an adventure that will not only open your eyes to its beauty but also touch your heart and leave an indelible mark on your soul. So, get ready to uncover the hidden gems of Nicaragua as we dive deeper into this land of enchantment in the following chapters.

Geographical and Cultural Highlights:

Geographical Highlights:

Nicaragua's geographical location makes it a captivating destination for nature lovers and adventure seekers. Bordered by Honduras to the north and Costa Rica to the south, the country boasts a strategic position in Central America. To the west, Nicaragua is caressed by the Pacific Ocean, offering a stunning coastline with a range of picturesque beaches. The eastern region is embraced by the Caribbean Sea, where pristine waters and untouched islands await exploration.

The Pacific Coast is a true paradise for beach enthusiasts. Stretching for hundreds of kilometers, it features a variety of coastal landscapes, from sandy stretches ideal for sunbathing and leisurely walks to rocky coves perfect for snorkeling and exploring marine life. Beach towns like San Juan del Sur and Tola have gained international acclaim for their laid-back atmosphere, breathtaking sunsets, and world-class surf breaks that attract surfers from all over the globe.

Venturing inland, Nicaragua's geography transitions to lush rainforests, expansive lakes, and towering volcanoes. The eastern region is characterized by dense jungles and tropical rainforests, home to a diverse array of plant and animal species. Nicaragua's crown jewel, Lake Nicaragua, is the largest freshwater lake in Central America and is dotted with volcanic islands, providing a unique setting for exploration and relaxation.

Cultural Highlights:

The people of Nicaragua are known for their warm hospitality, friendliness, and pride in their cultural heritage. A harmonious blend of indigenous, European, and African influences shapes the country's cultural landscape, infusing it with richness and diversity.

Nicaragua's indigenous heritage is deeply rooted in the traditions and customs of the pre-Columbian civilizations that once thrived in the region. The indigenous communities maintain their ancestral practices, arts, and crafts, offering visitors a glimpse into their ancient traditions and way of life.

The colonial era introduced European influences to Nicaragua, leaving a lasting impact on its architecture, language, and traditions. The colonial cities of Granada and León serve as living testaments to Nicaragua's colonial past, with their beautifully preserved buildings, cobblestone streets, and grand cathedrals. Exploring these cities provides a window into the country's historical significance and architectural splendor.

African influences can be traced back to the days of slavery, when Africans were brought to Nicaragua and contributed to the country's cultural tapestry. African rhythms and dances are still celebrated during vibrant festivals, adding a rhythmic heartbeat to the local culture.

Nicaragua's cultural fusion is evident in its art, music, and cuisine. Local artists create vibrant paintings, intricate pottery, and beautiful handicrafts that reflect the country's diverse heritage. Traditional music, such as marimba and folkloric tunes, fills the air during festivals and celebrations. Nicaraguan cuisine is a delightful blend of flavors, with dishes featuring staple ingredients like corn, beans, plantains, and fresh seafood.

As you explore Nicaragua, you'll have the opportunity to immerse yourself in this vibrant culture. Engage in conversations with locals, witness traditional dances and music performances, savor authentic Nicaraguan cuisine, and participate in cultural festivals that showcase the country's rich tapestry of traditions. The welcoming Nicaraguan people are eager to share their heritage with visitors, ensuring an immersive and unforgettable travel experience.

Why Visit Nicaragua?

Natural Beauty

One of the primary reasons why Nicaragua is a must-visit destination is its unparalleled natural beauty. The country is blessed with an astonishing array of landscapes that will leave you in awe. From majestic volcanoes to shimmering lakes, cascading waterfalls to dense tropical rainforests, Nicaragua offers a diverse tapestry of natural wonders that cater to every traveler's preferences.

If you're a nature lover, Nicaragua will delight you with its abundance of opportunities for exploration and adventure. Lace up your hiking boots and embark on thrilling hikes through lush cloud forests or challenging treks up towering volcanoes. Conquer the iconic peaks of volcanoes like Concepción on Ometepe Island or Mombacho near Granada, where you'll be rewarded with breathtaking panoramic views.

For those seeking tranquility and relaxation, Nicaragua's pristine beaches provide the perfect escape. The Pacific Coast is dotted with stunning stretches of sand, from the laid-back surfer havens of San Juan del Sur to the remote and untouched beaches of the Corn Islands in the Caribbean. Sink your toes into powdery white sands, soak up the sun, and let the rhythmic sound of crashing waves lull you into a state of bliss.

Waterfalls are another natural gem of Nicaragua, offering refreshing dips and awe-inspiring beauty. The La Maquina Waterfall in Matagalpa, with its cascading tiers surrounded by lush greenery, is a paradise for nature enthusiasts. The Somoto Canyon in the north of the country provides a unique opportunity to hike, swim, and float along its majestic cliffs and crystal-clear waters.

Moreover, Nicaragua's tropical rainforests are teeming with biodiversity. Explore the pristine jungles of the Indio Maíz Biological Reserve or the Bosawás Biosphere Reserve, where you can encounter rare species of flora and fauna. Take a guided wildlife tour and spot howler monkeys swinging through the treetops, colorful toucans perched on branches, and elusive jaguars roaming their natural habitats.

In Nicaragua, the wonders of nature are at your fingertips, waiting to be explored and appreciated in all their splendor.

Rich History and Cultural Heritage

Nicaragua boasts a fascinating history that stretches back centuries, making it a captivating destination for history buffs and culture enthusiasts alike. From ancient indigenous civilizations to the colonial era and the modern-day revolution, the country's past has shaped its present and continues to influence its vibrant cultural tapestry.

Step back in time as you explore the well-preserved colonial cities of Granada and León. Stroll through the narrow cobblestone streets lined with colorful colonial buildings, adorned with intricate wrought-iron balconies and grand cathedrals. Granada, known as the Jewel of Nicaragua, offers a glimpse into the country's colonial past, with its architectural marvels and charming plazas. León, the cultural capital, boasts a rich intellectual and artistic heritage, evident in its museums, galleries, and universities.

To delve even deeper into Nicaragua's history, visit ancient archaeological sites such as the ruins of León Viejo, a UNESCO World Heritage site, where you can witness the remnants of the original Spanish colonial capital buried beneath volcanic ash. Explore the mysterious petroglyphs at Ometepe Island or venture to the ancient footprints preserved in volcanic mud at the El Hoyo archaeological site.

Nicaragua's history also intertwines with its revolutionary past. Learn about the Sandinista Revolution, which shaped the country's modern identity, at the Revolutionary Museum in León. Gain insight into the struggles and triumphs of the Nicaraguan people as they fought for independence and social change.

By immersing yourself in Nicaragua's rich history and cultural heritage, you'll develop a deeper understanding and appreciation for the country and its people. Each step you take through the pages of history will bring you closer to unraveling the captivating story of Nicaragua.

Adventure and Outdoor Activities

For adventure enthusiasts, Nicaragua is an absolute playground of thrilling activities and outdoor pursuits. The country's diverse terrain and abundance of natural resources provide the perfect setting for adrenaline-fueled adventures.

If you're a surfer or aspiring to catch a wave, Nicaragua's Pacific Coast offers some of the best breaks in Central America. Head to popular surf spots like Popoyo, Playa Maderas, or Playa Hermosa, where consistent swells and warm waters attract surfers from around the world. Whether you're a seasoned pro or a beginner, there are surf schools and rental shops available to cater to all skill levels.

For a truly unique experience, venture inland to the volcanic landscapes of Nicaragua. Hiking up an active volcano is an unforgettable adventure that combines thrilling exertion with awe-inspiring natural beauty. Cerro Negro, known as the "Black Hill," near León, offers the opportunity to hike up its ash-covered slopes and then slide down on a sandboard, creating an adrenaline rush like no other.

Nicaragua's lakes and waterways provide excellent opportunities for kayaking and paddleboarding. Glide through the calm waters of Lake Nicaragua, the largest lake in Central America, and marvel at the picturesque islands scattered throughout. Explore the channels of the Río San Juan, where you can navigate through lush rainforests and encounter diverse wildlife along the riverbanks.

The country's national parks and reserves are a haven for outdoor enthusiasts seeking wildlife encounters and nature immersion. Indulge in a wildlife safari in the Bosawás Biosphere Reserve, home to a vast array of species including jaguars, tapirs, and colorful birds. Embark on a birdwatching expedition in the Rio San Juan Biosphere Reserve, where you can spot numerous migratory and endemic bird species.

From zip-lining through the treetops of the Mombacho Cloud Forest to horseback riding along the sandy shores of the Pacific, Nicaragua offers endless opportunities for adventure and outdoor activities. So, unleash your inner thrill-seeker and get ready to embrace the exhilaration that awaits in this playground of natural wonders.

Cultural Immersion

Nicaragua is a country brimming with vibrant culture and traditions, providing visitors with a unique opportunity to immerse themselves in a living cultural tapestry. From traditional music and dance to delectable cuisine and captivating festivals, Nicaragua offers a sensory feast for cultural enthusiasts.

One of the best ways to immerse yourself in Nicaraguan culture is through its cuisine. Sample authentic dishes like gallo pinto, a traditional breakfast of rice and beans, accompanied by plantains and cheese. Indulge in vigorón, a flavorful combination of yuca (cassava), cabbage slaw, and tender pork. Explore the local markets where you can taste an array of street food delicacies, such as nacatamales (savory corn dough filled with meat and vegetables) or baho (a slow-cooked meat dish).

Throughout the year, Nicaragua celebrates a vibrant calendar of festivals and celebrations that showcase its rich traditions. Witness the colorful processions and lively music during Semana Santa (Holy Week) in cities like León and Granada, where the streets come alive with religious fervor. Experience the joyous atmosphere of La Purísima, a December festival dedicated to the Virgin Mary, with families opening their homes to friends and neighbors for prayer and festive gatherings.

Music and dance are integral parts of Nicaraguan culture. The sounds of marimba, guitar, and traditional instruments fill the air as folkloric dances bring traditional stories to life. From the energetic Palo de Mayo dance in the Caribbean coast to the graceful El Güegüense, a satirical theater performance dating back to the colonial era, the rhythms and movements will captivate your senses.

Engage with local artisans and craftsmen to witness their creativity and skill firsthand. Visit pottery workshops in San Juan de Oriente, where skilled artisans mold clay into intricate masterpieces. Explore the artisan markets of Masaya, where you can find colorful handwoven textiles, beautiful wood carvings, and exquisite jewelry.

By immersing yourself in Nicaragua's vibrant culture, you'll forge connections with the local people and gain a deeper appreciation for the country's rich heritage. Embrace the warmth and hospitality of the Nicaraguan people as you uncover the hidden gems of their cultural tapestry.

As you embark on your Nicaraguan adventure, prepare to be captivated by its natural beauty, intrigued by its history, and embraced by its warm hospitality. Whether you're seeking relaxation, adventure, cultural immersion, or a combination of all three, Nicaragua promises to be an unforgettable destination that will leave a lasting impression on your heart and soul. Get ready to uncover the hidden gems of Central America's jewel as we dive deeper into the wonders of Nicaragua in the following chapters.

Getting Started

Essential Travel Information

Before embarking on your journey to Nicaragua, it is essential to familiarize yourself with some important travel information. This section provides you with the necessary details to ensure a smooth and enjoyable trip.

Visa Requirements and Entry Regulations:

When planning your trip to Nicaragua, it is crucial to understand the visa requirements based on your nationality. Nicaragua has specific entry regulations that vary depending on your country of origin. Some travelers may need to obtain a visa in advance, while others may be eligible for visa-free entry or visa on arrival.

To determine your specific visa requirements, visit the official website of the Nicaraguan embassy or consulate in your home country. There, you will find detailed information regarding the visa application process, required documents, fees, and processing times. It is recommended to initiate the visa application well in advance to allow for any necessary processing time.

In addition to the visa requirements, familiarize yourself with the entry regulations of Nicaragua. These regulations include passport validity requirements, which typically state that your passport should be valid for at least six months beyond your planned departure date from Nicaragua. Ensure that your passport meets these criteria to avoid any issues upon arrival.

When you arrive in Nicaragua, you will need to present your passport and any other required documents at immigration. It is essential to have all the necessary paperwork prepared in advance to streamline the entry process. Common documents required at immigration include a completed arrival/departure form (usually provided during your flight), proof of onward or return travel, and accommodation details.

Best Time to Visit Nicaragua:

Understanding the climate and weather patterns in Nicaragua is essential when determining the best time to visit. Nicaragua experiences a tropical climate with two distinct seasons: the dry season (November to April) and the rainy season (May to October). Each season offers unique advantages depending on your preferred activities and interests.

During the dry season, which is also the peak tourist season, you can expect sunny and dry weather across the country. This is an ideal time for outdoor adventures, such as hiking, surfing, and exploring the stunning beaches. The dry season provides excellent conditions for exploring nature reserves, national parks, and engaging in water sports along the Pacific and Caribbean coasts.

The rainy season, although characterized by frequent showers, can still be an attractive time to visit Nicaragua. The countryside flourishes with lush greenery, and the rainfall typically occurs in short bursts, leaving ample time for exploration. It is worth noting that some regions, especially along the Caribbean coast, experience heavier rainfall during this season. However, the rain can also bring about beautiful landscapes and fewer crowds, making it a quieter and more affordable time to visit.

When planning your visit, consider your preferred activities and interests. If you are primarily interested in water-based activities, such as surfing or snorkeling, the dry season may be more suitable. On the other hand, if you are drawn to the vibrant landscapes and are willing to embrace occasional showers, the rainy season can offer a unique and rewarding experience.

Health and Safety:

Before traveling to Nicaragua, it is important to research any recommended vaccinations or health precautions to ensure your well-being during your trip. Consult with your healthcare provider or a travel clinic well in advance of your departure to receive up-to-date medical advice and vaccinations.

Common vaccinations for Nicaragua may include hepatitis A and B, typhoid, tetanus, diphtheria, and influenza. The specific vaccinations required may vary based on factors such as your immunization history, the duration of your stay, and the regions you plan to visit within Nicaragua. It is advisable to schedule a medical appointment at least six weeks before your departure to allow sufficient time for vaccinations to take effect.

In addition to vaccinations, it is important to consider other health precautions. This may include using insect repellent to protect against mosquito-borne diseases like dengue fever and chikungunya. It is also advisable to drink bottled or purified water and practice good hygiene to avoid gastrointestinal issues.

When it comes to safety, staying informed about the current situation in Nicaragua is crucial. Stay updated on travel advisories issued by your country's foreign affairs department or embassy. These advisories provide valuable information about any potential safety risks, political situations, or specific regions that may require caution.

While Nicaragua is generally considered safe for tourists, it is always recommended to exercise common sense and take basic precautions. Be vigilant with your personal belongings, particularly in crowded areas or tourist hotspots. It is advisable to use reputable transportation services, especially for long-distance travel, and to avoid walking alone at night in unfamiliar areas.

Currency and Money Matters:

The official currency of Nicaragua is the Nicaraguan córdoba (NIO). It is essential to familiarize yourself with the local currency and understand the current exchange rate before your trip. You can exchange foreign currency into córdobas at banks, exchange offices, or authorized currency exchange locations.

It is advisable to have a mix of payment options for convenience. Cash is widely accepted in Nicaragua, particularly in smaller establishments, local markets, and rural areas. Ensure you have sufficient cash, especially if you plan to visit remote regions where ATM access may be limited.

ATMs are widely available in major cities and tourist areas, allowing you to withdraw cash in the local currency using your debit or credit card. However, it is important to notify your bank about your travel plans to prevent any potential issues with card usage abroad.

Credit cards, such as Visa and Mastercard, are generally accepted in larger hotels, restaurants, and established businesses. However, it is always recommended to carry some cash for smaller establishments or in case of any technical difficulties with card payment systems.

Language and Communication:

The official language of Nicaragua is Spanish. While English may be spoken to some extent in tourist areas and larger cities, it is beneficial to learn a few basic phrases in Spanish. This can greatly enhance your interactions with locals and make your travel experience more enjoyable.

Consider learning simple greetings, phrases for ordering food, asking for directions, and expressing gratitude. Nicaraguans appreciate the effort to communicate in their language and will often be more receptive and helpful.

In tourist areas and hotels, you are more likely to encounter English-speaking personnel who can assist you with general inquiries and provide guidance. However, it is always helpful to carry a pocket-sized Spanish phrasebook or have a translation app on your smartphone for situations where English may not be widely spoken.

When it comes to communication, Nicaragua has a reliable mobile network coverage, particularly in urban areas. Major telecommunication providers offer prepaid SIM cards for purchase, allowing you to have local connectivity and access to data services during your stay. Wi-Fi is also available in many hotels, cafes, and restaurants, although the signal strength and reliability may vary.

Customs and Etiquette:

To ensure respectful interactions with the Nicaraguan people, it is important to gain insights into the local customs and etiquette. Nicaraguans are known for their warmth, friendliness, and hospitality, and being aware of their cultural norms can help you navigate social situations with ease.

Common greetings in Nicaragua involve a handshake and direct eye contact. It is customary to greet individuals with "Buenos días" (good morning), "Buenas tardes" (good afternoon), or "Buenas noches" (good evening/night), depending on the time of day.

When addressing others, it is polite to use formal titles, such as "Señor" (Mr.), "Señora" (Mrs.), or "Señorita" (Miss), followed by the person's last name. In more casual settings, using first names is acceptable once a rapport has been established.

Nicaraguans value personal space and may stand slightly closer during conversations compared to some Western cultures. This proximity is not considered intrusive but rather a reflection of the warmth and familiarity within the culture.

It is customary to greet and say goodbye to each person individually when entering or leaving a group setting. Taking the time to acknowledge and bid farewell to each individual demonstrates respect and appreciation.

Nicaraguans have a strong sense of family and community. It is common to prioritize social interactions and engage in conversations beyond just the topic at hand. Take the time to show genuine interest in getting to know the people you encounter and engage in polite conversation.

When visiting religious sites or participating in cultural events, it is important to dress modestly and respectfully. Revealing clothing or attire that may be deemed offensive or inappropriate should be avoided out of respect for the local customs and religious practices.

By understanding and respecting the customs and etiquette of Nicaragua, you will be able to build positive connections with the locals and create memorable experiences during your journey. Remember that cultural sensitivity and open-mindedness go a long way in fostering meaningful interactions.

Visa Requirements and Entry Regulations

Visa Exemptions:

Nicaragua offers visa exemptions to citizens of certain countries, allowing them to enter the country without obtaining a visa in advance. This streamlined entry process facilitates travel and encourages tourism. The following section outlines the countries whose citizens can enter Nicaragua without a visa and provides information on the duration of their allowed stay.

Citizens from many countries, including the United States, Canada, the United Kingdom, Australia, and most European Union nations, can enter Nicaragua as tourists without a visa. These travelers are granted a tourist card upon arrival, which allows them to stay in the country for up to 90 days. It's important to note that the length of stay may vary for some nationalities, so it's recommended to check with the Nicaraguan embassy or consulate in your home country for the most up-to-date information.

Tourist Visa:

For travelers coming from countries that require a tourist visa to enter Nicaragua, this section provides detailed information on the application process, required documents, and fees involved. The tourist visa is suitable for those visiting Nicaragua for tourism, leisure, or visiting friends and family. It's essential to obtain the tourist visa before traveling to Nicaragua to ensure a smooth entry at the immigration checkpoint.

To apply for a tourist visa, you will need to submit the following documents:

- Completed visa application form.
- Valid passport with a minimum of six months validity beyond the intended stay.
- Passport-sized photographs.
- Proof of travel itinerary, including flight bookings and accommodation reservations.
- Proof of sufficient funds to cover your expenses during the stay.
- Visa fee payment receipt.

The application process usually involves submitting the required documents to the Nicaraguan embassy or consulate in your home country. It's advisable to apply well in advance to allow for sufficient processing time.

Once approved, the tourist visa allows for a specified duration of stay in Nicaragua. As mentioned earlier, for most nationalities, this is up to 90 days. However, it's important to review the specific visa conditions to ensure compliance with the regulations.

If you wish to extend your stay beyond the initially permitted duration, it's possible to apply for a visa extension through the Nicaraguan immigration authorities. This process requires submitting an extension application along with supporting documents and payment of associated fees. The extension allows for a longer stay in Nicaragua, but it's important to apply before the expiration of your initial visa to avoid any penalties or complications.

Business Visa:

If your purpose of travel to Nicaragua is for business-related activities, this section provides guidance on obtaining a business visa. The business visa allows individuals to engage in business meetings, attend conferences or seminars, explore investment opportunities, or conduct research.

To apply for a business visa, the following requirements may apply:

- Completed visa application form.
- Valid passport with a minimum of six months validity beyond the intended stay.
- Passport-sized photographs.
- Invitation letter from the host company or organization in Nicaragua.
- Supporting documents demonstrating the purpose of the visit, such as business letters, conference invitations, or proof of investment.
- Proof of financial means to cover your expenses during the stay.
- Visa fee payment receipt.

The duration of stay permitted under a business visa may vary. It's important to review the visa conditions and consult with the Nicaraguan embassy or consulate in your home country for accurate information.

Student Visa:

For those planning to pursue studies in Nicaragua, this section outlines the procedures and documentation needed to apply for a student visa. Nicaragua offers educational opportunities for international students, and obtaining a student visa is a crucial step in the process.

To apply for a student visa, you may need to provide the following documents:

- Completed visa application form.
- Valid passport with a minimum of six months validity beyond the intended stay.
- Passport-sized photographs.
- Acceptance letter from a recognized educational institution in Nicaragua.
- Proof of financial means to cover tuition fees and living expenses.
- Medical insurance coverage during the stay in Nicaragua.
- Visa fee payment receipt.

It's important to note that the educational institution you plan to attend must be recognized by the Nicaraguan government. Before applying for a student visa, it's recommended to verify the accreditation of the institution and understand any additional requirements or procedures that may apply.

Work Visa:

If you intend to work in Nicaragua, this section provides information on the different types of work visas available and the application process. Working legally in Nicaragua requires obtaining the appropriate work visa and work permit.

The types of work visas available may include:

- Temporary Work Visa: This visa is suitable for individuals working in Nicaragua for a limited period, such as contractors, consultants, or project-based professionals.

- Permanent Work Visa: This visa is for individuals intending to work and reside in Nicaragua for an extended period. It's commonly used for employees hired by Nicaraguan companies or those starting their own businesses.

To apply for a work visa, the following requirements may apply:

- Completed visa application form.
- Valid passport with a minimum of six months validity beyond the intended stay.
- Passport-sized photographs.
- Letter of employment or contract from the Nicaraguan company or organization.
- Supporting documents demonstrating the need for foreign labor or specialized skills.
- Work permit issued by the Nicaraguan Ministry of Labor.
- Visa fee payment receipt.

The responsibilities of both employers and employees regarding work visas and permits are outlined in Nicaraguan labor laws. It's crucial to comply with these regulations to ensure a legal and smooth working experience in Nicaragua.

Entry Requirements:

This section covers general entry requirements for all travelers visiting Nicaragua, regardless of their visa type. Understanding these requirements helps ensure a seamless entry process and avoids any unnecessary complications.

- Passport Validity: Your passport should have a minimum validity of six months beyond the intended stay in Nicaragua. It's recommended to renew your passport if it is close to expiration.

- Arrival and Departure Procedures: Upon arrival in Nicaragua, you will need to present your passport, visa (if applicable), and other required documentation to the immigration authorities. Keep the arrival/departure card provided by the immigration officers safe, as it will be required during your departure.
- Customs Regulations: Familiarize yourself with the customs regulations of Nicaragua to ensure compliance. It's important to declare any restricted or prohibited items and understand the duty-free allowances for various goods.
- Health and Vaccination Requirements: Check if there are any specific health or vaccination requirements for entering Nicaragua. Some countries may require proof of vaccination against certain diseases such as yellow fever. It's recommended to consult with your healthcare provider or visit a travel clinic before your trip.

Visa Extensions and Renewals:

If you wish to extend your stay in Nicaragua beyond the initially permitted duration, it's possible to apply for a visa extension. This section provides guidance on the procedures, required documents, and any associated fees for extending your visa.

To apply for a visa extension, you will typically need to:

- Submit an extension application form.
- Provide a valid reason for the extension, such as tourism, business, or studies.

- Submit supporting documents, such as proof of sufficient funds, accommodation arrangements, or enrollment in a recognized educational institution.
- Pay the visa extension fee.

It's important to note that visa extensions are subject to approval, and it's recommended to apply before the expiration of your initial visa to avoid any penalties or complications. The length of the extension granted may vary depending on the circumstances and the discretion of the immigration authorities.

Overstaying and Penalties:

Understanding the consequences of overstaying your permitted duration in Nicaragua is crucial. This section outlines the potential penalties and fines for overstaying your visa and provides advice on how to avoid such situations.

If you overstay your visa in Nicaragua, you may be subject to fines and other penalties. The length of overstay and the applicable fees or penalties can vary. It's important to be aware of your visa's expiration date and take necessary actions to extend or renew it before it expires.

To avoid overstaying your visa:

- Be aware of the expiration date: Keep track of the duration of stay permitted under your visa and ensure you have a valid visa throughout your time in Nicaragua.
- Apply for extensions in advance: If you need to extend your stay, apply for a visa extension before your current visa expires to maintain legal status.

- Seek professional advice: If you have any concerns or uncertainties about your visa status or extension, consult with immigration experts or the Nicaraguan embassy or consulate in your home country for accurate information.

By understanding and complying with the visa regulations, you can avoid any complications or penalties associated with overstaying your permitted duration in Nicaragua.

Special Entry Permits and Requirements:

For individuals with specific circumstances, such as journalists, volunteers, or retirees, this section highlights any special entry permits or requirements that may apply to them. It provides information on the necessary documentation and procedures to ensure compliance with Nicaraguan regulations.

Journalists: Journalists visiting Nicaragua for work purposes may require special permits or accreditation. It's essential to contact the Nicaraguan embassy or consulate in your home country or the relevant Nicaraguan authorities to understand the specific requirements and procedures.

Volunteers: If you are planning to volunteer in Nicaragua, you may need to obtain the appropriate visa or entry permit based on the nature and duration of your volunteer work. Consult with the organization you will be volunteering with to understand the necessary requirements and procedures.

Retirees: Nicaragua offers retirement programs and benefits for foreign retirees. This section provides an overview of the requirements and procedures for retirees wishing to relocate to Nicaragua. It may include information on income requirements, residency permits, and benefits available to retirees.

Other Special Circumstances: Depending on your specific circumstances, such as diplomatic visits, religious missions, or humanitarian work, there may be additional permits or requirements. It's important to contact the Nicaraguan embassy or consulate and relevant authorities to obtain accurate and up-to-date information for your particular situation.

Complying with the special entry permits and requirements ensures a smooth entry process and legal status during your stay in Nicaragua. It's advisable to seek guidance from the appropriate authorities or consult with professionals experienced in dealing with these specific circumstances.

Understanding the visa requirements and entry regulations of Nicaragua is crucial for a successful and enjoyable trip to the country. This comprehensive guide has provided information on visa exemptions, tourist visas, business visas, student visas, work visas, entry requirements, visa extensions and renewals, overstaying penalties, and special entry permits.

By familiarizing yourself with these regulations, you can plan your trip effectively, ensure a smooth entry process, and comply with the Nicaraguan immigration laws. Remember to always verify the information with the Nicaraguan embassy or consulate in your home country or consult with relevant authorities for the most accurate and up-to-date visa information.

Proper preparation and adherence to the visa regulations will contribute to a stress-free and rewarding experience as you explore the beauty and cultural richness of Nicaragua.

Best Time to Visit Nicaragua

The best time to visit Nicaragua largely depends on your preferences and the activities you wish to engage in during your trip. Nicaragua has a tropical climate, characterized by distinct wet and dry seasons. Understanding the weather patterns can help you plan your visit accordingly.

Dry Season (November to April):

The dry season in Nicaragua, which extends from November to April, is widely regarded as the best time to visit this beautiful Central American country. During this period, Nicaragua experiences predominantly dry and sunny weather, creating ideal conditions for outdoor activities and exploration of its natural wonders. The temperatures during the dry season are warm but not excessively hot, ranging from the mid-70s°F (mid-20s°C) to low 90s°F (low 30s°C), depending on the region.

One of the key advantages of visiting Nicaragua during the dry season is the abundance of outdoor recreational opportunities. Whether you're interested in hiking, surfing, or simply lounging on the pristine beaches, the dry season offers optimal conditions to indulge in these activities. The Pacific coast, with its world-class surf breaks, attracts wave enthusiasts from around the globe during this time. The clear skies and calm waters make it an excellent period for diving, snorkeling, and other water sports as well.

Exploring Nicaragua's natural wonders is particularly rewarding during the dry season. The lush rainforests, national parks, and volcanic landscapes are more accessible, with well-defined trails and less mud. Hiking enthusiasts can embark on adventures to conquer the volcanic peaks like Momotombo, Concepción, and Maderas. These treks offer breathtaking views of the surrounding landscapes and crater lakes.

Furthermore, the dry season is an ideal time to visit the stunning archipelago of Corn Islands, located off the Caribbean coast of Nicaragua. The crystal-clear waters surrounding these islands are perfect for snorkeling, scuba diving, and fishing, providing visitors with unforgettable underwater experiences.

However, it is important to note that the dry season is the most popular time for tourism in Nicaragua. As a result, expect larger crowds of tourists and higher prices, especially during peak holiday periods such as Christmas, New Year, and Easter. It is advisable to make accommodation and travel arrangements well in advance to secure your preferred choices.

Rainy Season (May to October):

From May to October, Nicaragua experiences its rainy season, characterized by frequent afternoon showers and occasional heavy downpours. While the rain can affect certain activities and logistics, it also brings its own charm and unique experiences to visitors.

The rainy season is often referred to as the "green season" or "off-season." Despite the increased precipitation, Nicaragua's landscapes transform into lush, vibrant greenery during this time, creating breathtaking scenery. The countryside comes alive with blooming flowers, and the rainforests teem with life, making it an excellent period for nature enthusiasts and birdwatchers.

One advantage of visiting Nicaragua during the rainy season is the fewer crowds. With fewer tourists, you can explore popular attractions with more peace and tranquility. This includes the colonial cities of Granada and León, where you can wander through the colorful streets and admire the beautiful architecture without the hustle and bustle of peak tourist numbers.

While the rain may limit certain activities, such as hiking or visiting remote areas that require traversing muddy trails, it also provides a unique opportunity to witness the power and beauty of nature. The occasional heavy downpours can be quite dramatic, and the thunderstorms create a mesmerizing spectacle across the country's landscape.

During the rainy season, temperatures in Nicaragua are slightly cooler compared to the dry season, ranging from the mid-70s°F (mid-20s°C) to high 80s°F (around 30°C). The cooler temperatures, combined with the rain, provide relief from the heat and humidity of the region.

It's important to note that the intensity and frequency of rainfall can vary across different regions of Nicaragua. The Caribbean coast generally experiences more rainfall throughout the year compared to the Pacific coast. Additionally, the timing and duration of rainfall can be unpredictable, with some areas receiving more rain than others.

When planning a trip during the rainy season, it's recommended to pack appropriate rain gear, including a lightweight waterproof jacket, umbrella, and sturdy footwear. It's also advisable to check weather forecasts and be prepared for sudden changes in weather conditions.

Specific considerations for visiting Nicaragua:

Surfing: If you're a surfing enthusiast, the best time to visit Nicaragua would be during the dry season, especially between November and March. Nicaragua's Pacific coast is renowned for its world-class surf breaks, attracting surfers from around the globe. During the dry season, consistent swells and favorable surfing conditions prevail, making it an ideal time to catch some waves.

The Pacific coast of Nicaragua offers a diverse range of surf spots suitable for all skill levels, from beginners to experienced surfers. Some popular surfing destinations include San Juan del Sur, Popoyo, Playa Maderas, and Playa Colorado. These areas boast consistent offshore winds, warm water temperatures, and a variety of breaks, including beach breaks, point breaks, and reef breaks.

November to March is considered the prime time for surfing in Nicaragua due to several factors. First, the prevailing offshore winds create clean and groomed waves, ensuring excellent surfing conditions. Second, the swell consistency is high, providing surfers with reliable waves to ride. The swells during this period are typically generated by northern hemisphere winter storms, resulting in powerful and well-formed waves.

During the dry season, the water temperatures hover around the mid-70s°F to low 80s°F (mid-20s°C to high 20s°C), offering comfortable conditions for surfers. The weather is generally sunny with minimal rainfall, allowing for longer surfing sessions and maximizing your time in the water. It's worth noting that the dry season is a popular time for tourists, so popular surf breaks may be more crowded compared to other times of the year.

Wildlife and Birdwatching: Nicaragua's rainy season, particularly from May to October, presents a unique opportunity for wildlife and birdwatching enthusiasts. The rain rejuvenates the country's diverse ecosystems, resulting in lush green landscapes and increased wildlife activity. Nicaragua is home to a wide range of habitats, including rainforests, wetlands, cloud forests, and coastal areas, supporting a rich biodiversity of flora and fauna.

The rainy season provides ample food and water sources for animals, making it an excellent time to observe their natural behaviors. The forests come alive with the sounds of birds, monkeys, and other wildlife species. Many migratory birds visit Nicaragua during this time, adding to the already impressive birdwatching opportunities. Birdwatchers can spot various species, including parrots, toucans, hummingbirds, and the iconic resplendent quetzal.

Popular destinations for wildlife and birdwatching in Nicaragua include the Indio Maíz Biological Reserve, Mombacho Volcano Natural Reserve, Bosawás Biosphere Reserve, and Juan Venado Island Nature Reserve. These protected areas offer guided tours and hiking opportunities to explore the diverse ecosystems and encounter wildlife up close.

Volcano Trekking: Nicaragua is known for its impressive volcanic landscapes, and if you're interested in hiking volcanoes, the dry season is the preferred time to visit. Nicaragua is home to several volcanoes, both active and dormant, offering thrilling trekking experiences and rewarding views from the summits.

During the dry season, which extends from November to April, the trails leading to the volcanoes are generally more accessible. The drier conditions make the hiking paths firmer and less muddy, ensuring a safer and more enjoyable trekking experience. Clear skies during the dry season also enhance the panoramic views from the volcano summits, allowing you to fully appreciate the awe-inspiring landscapes.

Some notable volcanoes in Nicaragua that are popular for trekking include Masaya Volcano, Mombacho Volcano, Telica Volcano, and Cerro Negro. Each volcano offers a unique hiking experience, ranging from moderate hikes to more challenging treks. Along the way, you'll encounter volcanic craters, lava fields, and potentially witness volcanic activity, such as steam vents and sulfur gases.

It's important to note that volcano trekking can be physically demanding, and it's advisable to go with an experienced guide who can provide valuable insights and ensure your safety throughout the hike. Proper hiking gear, including sturdy footwear, sunscreen, a hat, and sufficient water and snacks, is essential for a successful volcano trekking adventure.

Cultural Festivals: Nicaragua is a country deeply rooted in vibrant traditions and cultural celebrations. Throughout the year, various festivals and events take place, providing a glimpse into the rich cultural heritage of the Nicaraguan people. If you want to immerse yourself in these lively celebrations, checking the festival calendar and planning your visit accordingly is recommended.

One of the most significant cultural events in Nicaragua is Semana Santa, also known as Holy Week, which takes place in April. This religious festival commemorates the passion, death, and resurrection of Jesus Christ and is celebrated with processions, reenactments, and religious ceremonies in different cities and towns across the country. The most elaborate Semana Santa celebrations can be witnessed in León, Granada, and Masaya.

Another notable festival in Nicaragua is the Santo Domingo Festival, held in the town of Managua in August. This colorful event pays homage to Santo Domingo de Guzmán, the patron saint of Managua. The festival features traditional dances, parades, music performances, fireworks, and a lively carnival atmosphere that showcases the vibrant cultural heritage of Nicaragua.

Throughout the year, you may also encounter local festivals celebrating harvest seasons, patron saints, and historical events. These festivals often involve traditional dances, music, food, and arts and crafts, offering visitors a chance to experience the authentic cultural traditions of Nicaragua.

Attending cultural festivals in Nicaragua provides a unique opportunity to interact with locals, witness traditional customs, and indulge in the flavors of Nicaraguan cuisine. It's advisable to plan your visit well in advance and make accommodation arrangements accordingly, as festivals often attract large crowds, and accommodations may fill up quickly.

Remember to respect local customs and traditions while participating in festivals, and be mindful of any specific guidelines or regulations provided by the organizers. Immersing yourself in Nicaragua's cultural festivals will undoubtedly leave you with lasting memories and a deeper appreciation for the country's rich cultural tapestry.

It's important to note that weather patterns can vary across different regions of Nicaragua. The Pacific coast tends to have a drier climate compared to the Caribbean coast, which receives more rainfall throughout the year.

Regardless of the season, it's advisable to pack lightweight and breathable clothing, sunscreen, a hat, and insect repellent. Don't forget to check the current weather conditions and consult local resources before finalizing your travel plans to ensure the most enjoyable experience in Nicaragua.

Exploring Nature's Treasures

Discovering Nicaragua's National Parks

Nicaragua's national parks are true gems, preserving the country's extraordinary natural beauty and diverse ecosystems. From fiery volcanic landscapes to lush rainforests teeming with wildlife, these parks offer a remarkable journey through Nicaragua's natural treasures. This section will delve deeper into two of the most captivating national parks: Masaya Volcano National Park and Indio Maíz Biological Reserve.

Masaya Volcano National Park:

Situated just a short drive from the capital city of Managua, Masaya Volcano National Park is a mesmerizing destination that allows visitors to witness the raw power of an active volcano. The park's main attraction is the mighty Masaya Volcano, one of the few volcanoes in the world where you can peer directly into the crater.

As you enter the park, a sense of awe washes over you as the massive volcanic cone looms before you. The sight of smoke rising from the crater adds to the mystique, a reminder that this volcano is alive and ever-changing. The park offers several hiking trails that wind through the volcanic landscape, providing stunning panoramic views of the surrounding countryside.

During your hike, you'll encounter rugged terrain and ancient lava flows, evidence of the volcano's tumultuous history. Along the way, knowledgeable guides will share insights into the geology, formation, and volcanic activity of Masaya. They'll regale you with tales of past eruptions, including the legendary outburst that earned the volcano the moniker "Mouth of Hell."

As the sun begins to set, a truly magical experience awaits. At nightfall, the park opens for a unique opportunity to witness the "Gates of Hell" phenomenon. The glowing lava illuminates the crater, casting an eerie orange glow across the landscape. It's a surreal and unforgettable sight, providing a glimpse into the power and majesty of the natural world.

Indio Maíz Biological Reserve:

Located in southeastern Nicaragua, the Indio Maíz Biological Reserve is a vast rainforest sanctuary that ranks as the largest in Central America. This pristine and biodiverse ecosystem is a paradise for nature enthusiasts and wildlife lovers. The reserve's untouched beauty and remote location create a haven for rare and endangered species.

As you venture deep into Indio Maíz, a symphony of sounds surrounds you. Howler monkeys call from the treetops, exotic birds fill the air with their melodious songs, and the rustling of foliage hints at hidden creatures. The lush canopy above blocks out much of the sunlight, creating a cool and refreshing atmosphere as you explore the reserve's network of trails.

The biodiversity of Indio Maíz is astounding. Jaguars, ocelots, and tapirs roam these rainforest corridors, showcasing the reserve's importance as a stronghold for big cat conservation. Keen-eyed visitors may also spot troops of spider monkeys swinging through the trees or sloths leisurely traversing the branches.

For bird enthusiasts, Indio Maíz is a true paradise. The reserve boasts a remarkable variety of avian species, from colorful toucans and macaws to elusive quetzals and hummingbirds. Guided birdwatching tours offer the opportunity to spot and identify these magnificent feathered creatures, all while immersing yourself in the vibrant sounds and sights of the rainforest.

As you navigate the reserve's waterways, the Rio San Juan beckons with its tranquil beauty. Boat tours allow you to explore the winding river, where caimans lurk in the shallows and river otters play in the currents. The river also serves as a vital migratory route for countless bird species, offering unique opportunities for birdwatching enthusiasts.

Indio Maíz is not merely a place to observe nature; it's a place to connect with it. Camping facilities within the reserve provide a chance to spend a night beneath the stars, surrounded by the symphony of nocturnal creatures. As darkness falls, the jungle comes alive with the chorus of frogs and the distant hoots of nocturnal birds.

Visiting national parks like Masaya Volcano and Indio Maíz is not only a breathtaking experience but also an opportunity to appreciate Nicaragua's commitment to environmental conservation. These protected areas serve as vital refuges for wildlife, ensuring that future generations can continue to marvel at the country's natural wonders.

Rainforests, Wildlife, and Biodiversity

Nicaragua, known as the "Land of Lakes and Volcanoes," is a treasure trove for nature enthusiasts, offering an extraordinary array of rainforests that showcase the country's rich biodiversity. From dense tropical jungles to misty cloud forests, these ecosystems provide a habitat for a staggering variety of flora and fauna, making Nicaragua a paradise for those seeking a deep connection with nature.

Bosawás Biosphere Reserve: Exploring the Untouched Rainforest

One of the crown jewels of Nicaragua's rainforests is the Bosawás Biosphere Reserve, an expansive protected area that spans over 20,000 square kilometers. Situated in the northeast region of the country, Bosawás is the largest biosphere reserve in Central America and holds incredible ecological significance. As you delve into this untouched rainforest, you'll be immersed in a world of remarkable natural wonders.

The dense vegetation of Bosawás is home to countless species of plants, mammals, and birds, making it a biodiversity hotspot. Towering trees, including massive ceibas and mahogany, reach for the sky, forming a lush canopy that shelters an intricate ecosystem below. Orchids, bromeliads, and other epiphytes cling to the branches, adding bursts of color to the green tapestry. The air is filled with the symphony of bird calls, from the haunting cries of the resplendent quetzal to the vibrant melodies of toucans and hummingbirds.

As you venture deeper into Bosawás, hidden waterfalls cascade down moss-covered rocks, creating serene spots of tranquility. Pristine rivers wind their way through the rainforest, inviting exploration and providing habitats for aquatic species. Marvel at the intricate networks of roots and vines that crisscross the forest floor, serving as homes for an astonishing variety of insects, reptiles, and amphibians.

Beyond the remarkable natural beauty, Bosawás is also home to indigenous communities who have preserved their cultural heritage and traditional ways of life. By interacting with these communities, you have the opportunity to learn about their sustainable practices, ancient wisdom, and the close relationship they maintain with the land. This unique encounter offers a glimpse into the harmonious coexistence between humans and nature, and the importance of preserving these precious rainforests for future generations.

Mombacho Cloud Forest: Mystical Beauty on Misty Slopes

Located near the colonial city of Granada, Mombacho Volcano beckons with its mist-shrouded slopes and mystical allure. Ascending the volcano leads you to the captivating realm of the Mombacho Cloud Forest, an enchanting ecosystem that thrives in the cool, moist conditions found at higher elevations.

As you make your way along the winding trails of Mombacho, you'll be captivated by the diverse array of flora that blankets the forest. The cloud forest is characterized by an abundance of epiphytes, including orchids, bromeliads, and mosses, which cling to every available surface, creating a verdant wonderland. The air is infused with the fragrant scent of the forest, and the symphony of birdsong fills the misty atmosphere.

While exploring Mombacho's trails, keep a keen eye out for the charismatic inhabitants of the cloud forest. Howler monkeys swing through the treetops, their roars echoing in the mist. Sloths, known for their slow and deliberate movements, may be spotted hanging from branches, blending in with the foliage. Vibrantly colored butterflies flit by, while reptiles and amphibians camouflage themselves amidst the leaf litter and dense undergrowth.

The diverse array of bird species in Mombacho is a delight for birdwatchers. Listen for the distinctive calls of the emerald toucanet, the resplendent trogon, and the elusive quetzal. These avian treasures add splashes of color to the emerald-green canopy, their feathers glistening in the filtered sunlight that pierces through the mist.

The Mombacho Cloud Forest Reserve offers a range of activities for visitors to immerse themselves in the wonders of this unique ecosystem. Guided hikes provide opportunities to learn about the ecological significance of the cloud forest and its delicate balance. Zip-lining adventures allow you to soar through the canopy, gaining a bird's-eye view of the forest below. Interpretive centers provide educational exhibits and insights into the biodiversity and conservation efforts in the region.

Nicaragua's rainforests, including the majestic Bosawás Biosphere Reserve and the mystical Mombacho Cloud Forest, offer unparalleled opportunities to witness the incredible diversity and natural beauty of the country. Whether you find yourself navigating pristine rivers and hidden waterfalls in Bosawás or hiking amidst the misty trails and vibrant flora of Mombacho, these rainforests will leave you awe-inspired and connected to the wonders of the natural world. Take the time to explore and cherish these remarkable ecosystems, ensuring their preservation for generations to come.

Beaches and Coastal Escapes

With two stunning coastlines, Nicaragua offers an array of beautiful beaches and coastal destinations that cater to different preferences. Whether you seek relaxation, water sports, or vibrant beach towns, Nicaragua's coastal escapes have something for everyone.

San Juan del Sur: Discover the laid-back charm of San Juan del Sur, a popular beach town known for its golden sands, surf breaks, and lively atmosphere. Nestled along the Pacific Ocean, this vibrant coastal town attracts travelers from around the world with its breathtaking beaches and vibrant beach culture.

San Juan del Sur boasts several picturesque beaches, each with its own unique charm. Playa San Juan del Sur, the main beach, stretches along the town's waterfront and serves as a hub of activity. Here, you can sink your toes into the soft golden sands, bask in the sun, and take refreshing dips in the Pacific waters. The beach is dotted with cozy beachfront bars and restaurants where you can enjoy a delicious meal or sip on a tropical cocktail while admiring the stunning ocean views.

For those seeking adventure, San Juan del Sur is a haven for water sports enthusiasts. The consistent waves and favorable wind conditions make it an ideal spot for surfing and kiteboarding. Whether you're a seasoned pro or a beginner looking to catch your first wave, there are surf schools and rental shops that cater to all levels of experience. Grab a board and hit the waves, feeling the rush of adrenaline as you ride the Pacific swells.

If fishing is your passion, San Juan del Sur offers excellent opportunities to embark on thrilling fishing excursions. Join a local fishing charter and venture out into the deep blue sea, where you can try your luck at catching prized game fish like marlin, sailfish, and dorado. Whether you're an experienced angler or a first-time fisherman, the local guides will ensure you have an unforgettable fishing experience.

When you're ready to take a break from the beach and explore further, San Juan del Sur offers a range of activities and attractions. Hike up to the iconic Christ of the Mercy statue, perched on a hilltop overlooking the town, and enjoy panoramic views of the coastline. Explore the nearby nature reserves and take guided wildlife tours to spot monkeys, birds, and other fascinating creatures that inhabit the surrounding forests.

After a day of sun, surf, and adventure, the lively nightlife of San Juan del Sur awaits. The town comes alive in the evenings with a vibrant atmosphere, bustling bars, and beachfront parties. Dance to the rhythm of Latin beats, mingle with fellow travelers, and create unforgettable memories as you immerse yourself in the energetic nightlife scene.

Corn Islands: Unwind on the pristine shores of the Corn Islands, located in the Caribbean Sea. Comprising Big Corn Island and Little Corn Island, these tropical paradises offer a tranquil and idyllic escape from the hustle and bustle of everyday life.

Big Corn Island, the larger of the two islands, is known for its laid-back atmosphere and stunning beaches. Walk along the powdery white sands, lapped by crystal-clear turquoise waters, and feel the warm embrace of the Caribbean sun.

Relax under the shade of swaying palm trees, sipping on a refreshing coconut or tropical drink.

Snorkeling and diving enthusiasts will be in awe of the vibrant underwater world that awaits them in the Corn Islands. Explore the vibrant coral reefs teeming with a kaleidoscope of tropical fish, sea turtles, and other fascinating marine life. The clear waters and excellent visibility make it a paradise for underwater photography and capturing the beauty of the aquatic ecosystem.

Little Corn Island, a smaller and more secluded island, offers a more rustic and off-the-grid experience. There are no cars on the island, and the pace of life is slow and unhurried. Meander along sandy pathways shaded by palm trees, and explore the island's pristine beaches, where you can find a secluded spot to relax and unwind.

Little Corn Island is renowned for its diving opportunities, with numerous dive shops offering courses and guided dives for all levels of experience. Dive into the depths of the Caribbean Sea and discover stunning coral formations, underwater caves, and encounters with majestic sea creatures such as nurse sharks and eagle rays.

In addition to its natural beauty, the Corn Islands boast a vibrant cultural heritage influenced by African, Indigenous, and Caribbean traditions. Sample the flavors of the islands by indulging in fresh seafood delicacies, including lobster, shrimp, and fish, prepared with local spices and culinary flair. Engage with the friendly locals, who are known for their warm hospitality, and learn about the islands' rich history and cultural traditions.

Whether you choose San Juan del Sur or the Corn Islands, Nicaragua's coastal destinations offer a mix of relaxation, adventure, and natural beauty. Whether you're seeking to ride the waves, bask in the sun, explore underwater wonders, or simply unwind on pristine beaches, Nicaragua's coastal escapes will leave you with unforgettable memories of tropical bliss.

Volcanic Landscapes and Adventure

Nicaragua, often referred to as the "Land of Lakes and Volcanoes," is a country blessed with a remarkable landscape shaped by its impressive volcanic activity. From thrilling adventures to breathtaking views, exploring the volcanic wonders of Nicaragua promises an unforgettable experience for nature enthusiasts and adventure seekers alike.

One of the most renowned volcanic destinations in Nicaragua is Cerro Negro, an active volcano located near the city of León. Standing proudly amidst a desolate landscape of black volcanic ash, Cerro Negro offers a unique opportunity for adrenaline junkies: volcano boarding. This exhilarating activity involves strapping on a specialized board and hurtling down the steep slopes of Cerro Negro, reaching speeds of up to 50 miles per hour. As you descend, the black ash kicks up around you, creating an adrenaline-fueled rush and a truly unforgettable adventure. Whether you're a seasoned thrill-seeker or simply seeking a one-of-a-kind experience, volcano boarding on Cerro Negro is bound to get your heart racing.

Another volcanic gem in Nicaragua is Ometepe Island, a natural marvel formed by two majestic volcanoes rising from the vast expanse of Lake Nicaragua. The twin volcanoes, Concepción and Maderas, dominate the island's landscape and provide a stunning backdrop for exploration. Ometepe

Island is a paradise for hikers and nature lovers, offering a diverse range of trails that wind through lush forests, revealing hidden treasures along the way.

For those seeking a challenge, a hike to the summit of Concepción Volcano presents a rewarding and awe-inspiring experience. The ascent is not for the faint of heart, as the steep and rugged terrain demands physical endurance and determination. However, reaching the summit is a feat that rewards hikers with panoramic views of Lake Nicaragua, the surrounding islands, and the lush greenery that blankets Ometepe. The sense of accomplishment and the breathtaking vistas make the journey worth every step.

If you prefer a less arduous adventure, Ometepe Island offers an abundance of other trails that cater to various fitness levels. Explore the trails that wind through the island's forests, revealing ancient petroglyphs etched into rocks by the island's indigenous inhabitants. Discover cascading waterfalls hidden amidst the verdant foliage, offering a refreshing respite and a chance to immerse yourself in the island's natural beauty.

Beyond the volcanic wonders, Ometepe Island boasts a rich cultural heritage and a warm, welcoming community. Explore the local villages, where you can engage with friendly residents, sample traditional Nicaraguan cuisine, and learn about the island's history and folklore. Discover the island's unique handicrafts, such as intricately woven hammocks and ceramic pottery, which reflect the artistic talents of the local artisans.

As you navigate Ometepe Island, you'll find that the volcanic landscapes and the tranquil beauty of Lake Nicaragua create a sense of harmony and serenity. The island's natural treasures and cultural richness make it a haven for ecotourism and sustainable travel, with various initiatives focused on preserving the island's unique ecosystem and supporting the local communities.

Whether you choose to conquer the challenging heights of Concepción Volcano or meander through the forested trails, Ometepe Island invites you to immerse yourself in its natural wonders and experience the captivating power of Nicaragua's volcanoes. With its dramatic landscapes, vibrant culture, and warm hospitality, Ometepe Island embodies the essence of Nicaragua, leaving an indelible mark on all who venture to its shores.

Cloud Forests and Resplendent Quetzals

Nicaragua's cloud forests are truly enchanting, offering a unique and mystical experience for nature lovers. These ethereal landscapes, shrouded in mist and teeming with life, provide a haven for various flora and fauna. One of the most coveted sightings in these forests is the resplendent quetzal, a bird revered for its dazzling plumage. Let's explore two remarkable cloud forest reserves in Nicaragua: El Jaguar Reserve and Tisey Nature Reserve.

El Jaguar Reserve:

Located in the mountains of northern Nicaragua, El Jaguar Reserve is a captivating cloud forest sanctuary that beckons adventurers and nature enthusiasts alike. As you embark on your journey through this reserve, be prepared to be awe-struck by the captivating beauty that surrounds you. The air is crisp, and the trails wind through a verdant landscape of ancient trees adorned with delicate drapes of moss and ferns.

Hiking through El Jaguar Reserve is like stepping into a fairytale. The mist veils the forest, creating an ethereal ambiance that adds to the sense of wonder. As you meander along the mist-shrouded trails, you'll feel a profound connection with nature. Each step reveals a new surprise, from vibrant flowers to hidden waterfalls cascading down moss-covered rocks.

One of the main highlights of El Jaguar Reserve is the opportunity to spot the resplendent quetzal. This elusive bird, with its iridescent emerald plumage and long, flowing tail feathers, is a symbol of beauty and grace. Keep your eyes peeled and your ears tuned to the forest's whispers as you search for this legendary creature. While the quetzal steals the spotlight, you'll also encounter other avian wonders such as toucans with their vibrant beaks and hummingbirds darting through the canopy.

The diverse ecosystem of El Jaguar Reserve extends beyond its avian inhabitants. The forest floor teems with life, with an array of colorful orchids, bromeliads, and ferns carpeting the ground. The biodiversity is astounding, with countless species of insects, reptiles, and mammals finding refuge within this pristine environment. Listen to the symphony of bird calls, the gentle rustling of leaves, and the occasional chatter of monkeys swinging through the trees.

Tisey Nature Reserve:

Nestled near the town of Estelí, Tisey Nature Reserve is a hidden gem waiting to be discovered. This cloud forest paradise captivates visitors with its cool climate, lush vegetation, and pristine waterfalls. As you enter Tisey, a sense of serenity washes over you, transporting you to a world untouched by time.

The cool mist envelops the forest, creating an ethereal atmosphere that is both calming and invigorating. Wander along the well-maintained trails that wind through the reserve, allowing you to immerse yourself fully in the natural beauty that surrounds you. The towering trees create a dense canopy, filtering the sunlight and casting a dappled glow on the forest floor.

One of the most remarkable aspects of Tisey Nature Reserve is its vibrant birdlife. The melodious calls of numerous bird species fill the air, making it a haven for birdwatchers. With patience and a keen eye, you may spot the endemic turquoise-browed motmot or the colorful montezuma oropendola, among many others. The reserve is also home to a variety of mammals, including howler monkeys and sloths, which can occasionally be spotted lounging in the treetops.

As you explore Tisey, be sure to take in the breathtaking waterfalls that punctuate the landscape. These natural wonders provide a soothing soundtrack as the crystal-clear waters cascade over moss-covered rocks, creating small pools that invite you to dip your feet and cool off. The sight and sound of the rushing water harmonize with the tranquility of the forest, creating a truly immersive experience.

Tisey Nature Reserve also boasts an impressive array of endemic plant species. Orchids in various shapes and colors adorn the trees, their delicate beauty adding an enchanting touch to the forest. As you traverse the trails, you'll encounter towering ferns, bromeliads, and epiphytes clinging to the branches, showcasing the resilience and adaptability of nature.

In addition to the natural wonders, Tisey Nature Reserve offers opportunities for cultural immersion. The reserve is surrounded by communities that maintain a strong connection to the land. Interact with the locals and learn about their traditions, such as traditional farming techniques or the production of artisanal crafts. Their deep appreciation for nature and the environment is evident in the way they preserve and respect this remarkable cloud forest sanctuary.

Islands and Marine Biodiversity

Beyond its mainland, Nicaragua is blessed with a collection of captivating islands and archipelagos that beckon travelers to explore the beauty of its Caribbean and Pacific coasts. These island getaways offer an escape to turquoise waters, abundant marine life, and pristine beaches, creating a paradise for nature enthusiasts and beach lovers alike.

One such jewel in the Caribbean Sea is the Pearl Cays, a stunning archipelago located off Nicaragua's Caribbean coast. This group of islands, named for the lustrous pearls once found in its waters, presents a maritime adventure like no other. As you set sail to the Pearl Cays, anticipation builds as the turquoise hues of the sea come into view, promising an extraordinary experience.

Upon arrival, immerse yourself in the crystal-clear waters teeming with life. Snorkeling or diving in the pristine coral reefs reveals a vibrant underwater world, where an array of colorful fish dance among the coral formations. The reef ecosystem here is a biodiversity hotspot, offering encounters with species such as parrotfish, angelfish, butterflyfish, and many more. Keep your eyes peeled for graceful sea turtles gliding through the water, as they are frequent visitors to these protected waters. If luck is on your side, you might even catch a glimpse of a gentle manatee, gracefully moving through the shallows.

When it's time to unwind, the Pearl Cays offers a collection of secluded white-sand beaches, providing the perfect setting for relaxation and rejuvenation. As you step onto the powdery sands, the cares of the world melt away. Find a quiet spot under the shade of a palm tree, feel the gentle sea breeze caress your skin, and listen to the soothing sounds of the waves. It's a serene oasis where you can truly disconnect from the outside world and immerse yourself in the tranquility of nature.

Moving to the Pacific coast, another natural wonder awaits: Juan Venado Island. This narrow island, located near the city of León, is a designated wildlife refuge and a haven for those seeking an intimate encounter with nature. Exploring Juan Venado Island feels like stepping into a hidden paradise, where mangrove forests line the shores and a diverse array of wildlife thrives.

Embark on a boat tour that takes you through the winding channels of the island's mangrove ecosystem. Glide silently along the water, allowing the peacefulness of the surroundings to envelop you. As you navigate through the maze of mangroves, keep your eyes peeled for the incredible bird species that call this place home. From magnificent frigatebirds soaring in the sky to herons and egrets gracefully wading through the shallows, the birdlife here is a spectacle to behold.

But it's not just the avian inhabitants that make Juan Venado Island special. Crocodiles lurk beneath the surface, their eyes and snouts visible as they bask in the sun. These ancient creatures add a touch of wildness to the island's ecosystem, reminding us of the delicate balance between predator and prey in nature.

One of the most remarkable aspects of Juan Venado Island is its role as a nesting ground for sea turtles. These majestic creatures return year after year to lay their eggs in the warm sands, continuing a timeless cycle of life. If you visit during the nesting season, you might witness the awe-inspiring sight of a sea turtle emerging from the waves, slowly making her way up the beach, and carefully digging a nest to deposit her eggs. Observing this natural phenomenon is an unforgettable experience, a testament to the resilience and beauty of these ancient mariners.

As you explore Juan Venado Island, you'll come to appreciate the importance of conservation efforts in preserving such pristine habitats. The island's status as a wildlife refuge serves as a sanctuary for the flora and fauna that thrive within its boundaries. It's a reminder of the delicate balance we must strike to protect these natural wonders for future generations to enjoy.

Whether you choose to explore the Pearl Cays' underwater paradise or immerse yourself in the tranquil beauty of Juan Venado Island, Nicaragua's islands and archipelagos offer a glimpse into the incredible diversity of the country's coastal ecosystems. From colorful reefs and marine life to mangrove forests and nesting sea turtles, these natural treasures captivate the hearts of all who venture to their shores. They invite you to disconnect from the world, connect with nature, and create memories that will last a lifetime.

Colonial Heritage and Historical Sites

Exploring Nicaragua's Colonial Cities

Nicaragua is home to several stunning colonial cities that showcase the country's rich history and architectural beauty. Embark on a journey through time as you explore these captivating destinations, each with its unique charm and stories to tell.

Granada: The Jewel of Nicaragua

Granada, known as the "Jewel of Nicaragua," is a city that transports visitors back in time with its well-preserved colonial architecture, vibrant colors, and captivating atmosphere. As you step onto the cobblestone streets, you'll be greeted by a visual feast of Spanish colonial buildings adorned with ornate facades, charming balconies, and enchanting courtyards. Here, every corner exudes history, and the city's undeniable charm beckons you to explore its treasures.

Parque Central:

At the heart of Granada lies Parque Central, a vibrant and bustling central park that serves as the social and cultural hub of the city. Surrounded by historical landmarks, cafes, and colorful buildings, this lively public space is a favorite gathering place for both locals and tourists alike. As you enter the park, you'll immediately feel the energy and excitement that fills the air.

Take a leisurely stroll through Parque Central, allowing yourself to be immersed in the vibrant atmosphere. The park is adorned with well-manicured gardens, tall shade trees, and inviting benches where you can relax and soak up the surroundings. You'll often find locals engaged in friendly chess matches, showcasing their skills and strategic thinking. It's not uncommon to witness passionate debates or lively conversations among friends and acquaintances. Street performers add an extra touch of entertainment, mesmerizing onlookers with their talents in music, dance, or even magic tricks.

Parque Central is also a hub for vendors who set up stalls to sell traditional snacks and handicrafts. Indulge in delicious treats like vigorón, a mouthwatering combination of yuca (cassava), chicharrón (fried pork rinds), and cabbage salad, or try some local fruits and freshly squeezed juices. As you savor these flavors, you can browse through the handicrafts on display, including intricately woven textiles, handmade jewelry, and beautiful pottery. It's an excellent opportunity to support local artisans and take home a unique piece of Granada's culture.

Catedral de Granada:

Dominating the city's skyline with its impressive yellow facade, the Catedral de Granada stands as a symbol of Granada's rich religious heritage and architectural splendor. This magnificent cathedral, dating back to the 16th century, is one of the oldest in Central America and holds great historical and cultural significance.

Step inside the Catedral de Granada, and you'll be awestruck by its grandeur and beauty. The interior boasts intricate architectural details, including ornate wooden altars, exquisite stained glass windows that cast colorful hues across the space, and religious artwork that tells stories of faith and devotion. As you explore the cathedral, you can't help but feel a sense of reverence and admiration for the craftsmanship and artistry that went into its construction.

The cathedral is not just a place of worship; it also serves as a cultural and historical landmark. It has witnessed the city's growth, weathered various challenges, and stood as a symbol of strength and resilience. Attending a religious service or a special event at the Catedral de Granada offers a unique opportunity to witness the religious practices and traditions of the local community.

La Calzada Street:

For food lovers, shoppers, and nightlife enthusiasts, La Calzada is a vibrant and bustling pedestrian street that should not be missed. As you step onto La Calzada, you'll be greeted by a lively atmosphere filled with the aromas of delicious food, the sounds of music, and the laughter of people enjoying themselves.

The street is lined with a myriad of restaurants, bars, and shops, offering a diverse range of culinary delights, unique souvenirs, and locally made crafts. Indulge in Nicaraguan cuisine as you dine at one of the charming restaurants, sampling traditional dishes such as gallo pinto, a flavorful combination of rice and beans, or baho, a succulent meat stew cooked with plantains and vegetables. Enjoy the blend of flavors and spices that make Nicaraguan cuisine so enticing.

As you explore the shops along La Calzada, you'll find a treasure trove of handicrafts, artwork, and clothing. Look out for intricately woven textiles, vibrant paintings depicting local scenes, and handmade jewelry that showcases the skill and creativity of Nicaraguan artisans. It's a perfect opportunity to find unique souvenirs to commemorate your visit and support the local economy.

As the sun sets, La Calzada truly comes alive with its vibrant nightlife. Live music performances fill the air, and the street transforms into a lively hub of entertainment. Dance to the rhythm of salsa or merengue, or simply sit back and enjoy the ambiance while sipping a refreshing cocktail or trying a local craft beer. The lively atmosphere, combined with the opportunity to mingle with both locals and fellow travelers, creates an unforgettable experience on La Calzada.

Isletas de Granada:

A short boat ride from Granada lies the Isletas de Granada, an archipelago of small islands scattered throughout the majestic Lake Nicaragua. This natural paradise offers a serene and tranquil escape from the bustling city.

Embark on a boat tour and navigate through the intricate waterways that wind their way through the Isletas. Each island has its unique charm, with lush vegetation, exotic wildlife, and breathtaking views of the surrounding landscape. Marvel at the sight of the majestic Mombacho Volcano towering in the distance, adding a touch of grandeur to the picturesque scenery.

As you explore the Isletas, keep your eyes peeled for the abundant bird species that call this area home. The islands provide a sanctuary for a variety of avian life, and birdwatching enthusiasts will be delighted by the opportunity to spot colorful toucans, graceful herons, and playful monkeys swinging through the treetops.

For those seeking relaxation, the Isletas offer a peaceful retreat. Take a refreshing swim in the crystal-clear waters of the lake, feeling the gentle caress of the warm sun on your skin. Find a secluded spot on one of the islands, and simply bask in the tranquility, surrounded by the beauty of nature.

Exploring Granada:

While Parque Central, the Catedral de Granada, La Calzada, and the Isletas are highlights of Granada, there is so much more to discover in this enchanting city. Lose yourself in the narrow streets and alleys, where every turn reveals another architectural gem or a hidden courtyard filled with tropical plants. Explore the Convento y Museo San Francisco, a former convent turned museum, housing an impressive collection of religious art and artifacts. Climb to the top of the Iglesia La Merced bell tower for panoramic views of the city and its surroundings. Wander along the Malecón, a promenade along the shores of Lake Nicaragua, offering breathtaking vistas and a chance to relax in the lakeside parks.

During your visit to Granada, be sure to immerse yourself in the city's rich history and culture. Engage in conversations with locals, who are often eager to share stories about their city's heritage and traditions. Experience the warmth and hospitality of Nicaraguan people as you explore the markets, engage in cultural events, and perhaps even participate in a traditional dance or music performance. Granada is a city that invites you to connect with its past, embrace its present, and create lasting memories of your journey through its streets and beyond.

Granada's charm extends beyond its physical beauty. It embodies the soul of Nicaragua, offering a unique blend of history, culture, and natural wonders. Whether you're exploring the colonial streets, indulging in the local cuisine, or admiring the natural landscapes, Granada is a destination that will captivate your senses and leave an indelible mark on your travel memories.

León: Cultural Capital and Revolutionary History

León, often hailed as the cultural capital of Nicaragua, is a city that exudes history, art, and intellectual heritage. Located in the western part of the country, León offers a glimpse into Nicaragua's rich cultural tapestry, boasting magnificent churches, a renowned university, and a strong connection to the country's revolutionary past.

Highlights of León:

León Cathedral:

A visit to León would be incomplete without exploring the awe-inspiring León Cathedral, a true architectural marvel. Recognized as a UNESCO World Heritage Site, the cathedral stands proudly as the largest cathedral in Central America. Its imposing facade, adorned with intricate carvings and statues, is a testament to the city's colonial heritage. Step inside to marvel at the grandeur of the interior, with its soaring arches, ornate altars, and beautiful stained glass windows. Ascend to the rooftop for panoramic views of the city and surrounding landscapes, offering a unique perspective of León's historical charm.

Museo de la Revolución:

Immerse yourself in Nicaragua's revolutionary history by visiting the Museo de la Revolución. Housed in a former political prison, this museum provides a compelling glimpse into the Sandinista Revolution, which transformed the country in the late 20th century. Explore the exhibits filled with artifacts, photographs, and personal accounts, which shed light on the struggle for social justice and the fight against dictatorship. Gain a deeper understanding of the revolutionary movement that shaped modern Nicaragua and left a lasting impact on its people.

Rubén Darío Museum:

Step into the world of Rubén Darío, Nicaragua's most celebrated poet, at the Rubén Darío Museum. Located in the poet's former residence, this museum offers a captivating journey through Darío's life and literary contributions. Delve into the poet's works, manuscripts, personal belongings, and correspondence, gaining insight into the artistic and intellectual landscape of his time. The museum pays homage to Darío's significant influence on Latin American literature and his role in the modernist movement.

León Viejo:

For a glimpse into Nicaragua's colonial past, venture to León Viejo, the archaeological site of the original colonial city. Buried by volcanic ash in the 17th century, this UNESCO World Heritage Site offers a fascinating window into the lives of early settlers. Stroll through the well-preserved ruins, including the foundations of homes, churches, and public buildings. Learn about the city's historical significance and the challenges it faced from volcanic activity. As you explore the site, imagine the bustling streets and vibrant community that once thrived in this colonial hub.

Beyond the Highlights:

León offers much more to explore beyond its iconic landmarks. The city's streets are adorned with vibrant murals, showcasing the talent and creativity of local artists. Take a leisurely walk through the colorful barrios, admiring the artistic expressions that depict Nicaragua's history, culture, and social issues. Visit the lively Mercado Central, where the sights, sounds, and scents of local life converge. Engage with vendors, taste traditional Nicaraguan dishes, and discover unique handicrafts.

León's vibrant cultural scene is also enhanced by its prestigious university, Universidad Nacional Autónoma de Nicaragua (UNAN). The university has long been a hub for intellectual pursuits, nurturing the minds of renowned poets, writers, and scholars. Take a stroll through the university campus, and soak in the youthful energy and academic atmosphere that permeate the city.

As you navigate the streets of León, you'll encounter numerous opportunities to engage with the local community. Strike up conversations with friendly locals, who are often eager to share stories about their city's heritage and traditions. Discover hidden art galleries, attend poetry readings, or enjoy live music performances that reflect the city's artistic spirit.

León's cultural capital and revolutionary history make it a captivating destination for travelers seeking a deeper understanding of Nicaragua's past and present. From its magnificent cathedral to its museums and archaeological sites, the city offers a rich tapestry of experiences that will leave a lasting impression on your journey through this remarkable country.

Other Historical Sites and Landmarks

In addition to Granada and León, Nicaragua boasts several other historical sites and landmarks that provide insights into the country's past and cultural heritage.

Masaya: A City of Crafts and Folklore

Masaya Artisan Market:

The Masaya Artisan Market is a vibrant and bustling hub of creativity and craftsmanship located in the city of Masaya, Nicaragua. This market is a treasure trove for those seeking unique and authentic Nicaraguan handicrafts. As you enter the market, you'll be greeted by a kaleidoscope of colors, the aroma of freshly brewed coffee, and the sounds of artisans at work.

The market is renowned for its wide array of traditional handicrafts, showcasing the artistic talents of local artisans. Wander through the maze-like corridors and explore the stalls brimming with pottery, textiles, woodcarvings, and other handcrafted items. Admire the intricate designs and patterns that reflect Nicaragua's cultural heritage and indigenous traditions.

Pottery holds a special place in Nicaraguan culture, and you'll find an abundance of beautifully crafted ceramics at the market. From ornate vases and decorative plates to traditional cooking pots, each piece tells a story and represents the artistic prowess of the local artisans. Marvel at the delicate brushwork and vibrant colors used in the creation of these pottery masterpieces.

Textiles are another highlight of the Masaya Artisan Market. Browse through racks of handwoven hammocks, intricately embroidered clothing, and colorful tapestries. These textiles showcase the craftsmanship and skills passed down through generations. Feel the softness of the fabrics and appreciate the attention to detail that goes into creating these textile treasures.

Woodcarvings are yet another specialty of the market. Intricately carved masks, figurines, and decorative pieces display the incredible talent and dedication of Nicaraguan woodworkers. From traditional religious motifs to whimsical animal sculptures, each woodcarving is a work of art that reflects the cultural heritage and nature of Nicaragua.

As you interact with the artisans, you'll have the opportunity to learn about their craft techniques and the stories behind their creations. Many artisans are happy to share their knowledge and passion for their work, allowing you to gain a deeper appreciation for the artistry involved.

Masaya Volcano National Park:

A short distance from the city of Masaya lies the awe-inspiring Masaya Volcano National Park. This natural wonder is home to Masaya Volcano, an active volcano that offers a mesmerizing display of nature's power and beauty. As you approach the park, you'll be greeted by the sight of the volcano's plume of smoke rising against the sky, creating an otherworldly atmosphere.

At the park, you can embark on a journey to witness the grandeur of Masaya Volcano firsthand. The main attraction is the Santiago Crater, a stunning volcanic crater that emits smoke and gases. Standing at the edge of the crater, you'll be captivated by the sight of the molten lava glowing within, creating an ethereal spectacle.

To fully appreciate the volcanic wonders, take a guided tour that will lead you along well-maintained trails, providing informative insights about the geological significance of the area. As you explore, you'll be surrounded by unique flora and fauna that have adapted to the volcanic environment.

For a more immersive experience, consider visiting the park during sunset. As the day draws to a close, the sky transforms into a canvas of vibrant hues, setting the stage for a breathtaking view of the volcano against the backdrop of the colorful sky. The play of light and shadows creates a surreal ambiance, offering a truly unforgettable experience.

It's important to note that while Masaya Volcano is active, it is closely monitored for safety. Park rangers ensure that visitors can witness the volcano's splendor while maintaining a safe distance. As with any volcanic activity, it's essential to follow the guidance and regulations provided by the park authorities.

The Masaya Volcano National Park is not only a geological marvel but also a significant cultural and historical site. It holds great importance to the local indigenous communities who have revered and respected the volcano for centuries. Exploring this natural wonder allows you to connect with Nicaragua's unique volcanic heritage and gain a deeper understanding of the country's geological and cultural identity.

Visiting the Masaya Artisan Market and Masaya Volcano National Park offers a diverse and enriching experience in Nicaragua. From immersing yourself in the creativity and craftsmanship of local artisans to witnessing the raw power of an active volcano, these attractions allow you to delve into the rich cultural and natural heritage of the region. Whether you're seeking handcrafted souvenirs or seeking a deeper appreciation for the wonders of nature, these destinations will leave an indelible impression on your Nicaraguan journey.

Ometepe Island: Nature and Archaeology

Nestled in the vast waters of Lake Nicaragua, Ometepe Island is a true natural wonder. Shaped by two majestic volcanoes, Concepción and Maderas, the island offers visitors a mesmerizing blend of lush landscapes, pristine beaches, and intriguing archaeological sites. As you set foot on Ometepe, prepare to be enchanted by its raw beauty and rich cultural heritage.

The island's formation is a geological marvel, resulting from past volcanic activity that sculpted the landscape into what it is today. Rising dramatically from the center of Lake Nicaragua, Concepción stands tall as a formidable volcano, while Maderas, draped in dense rainforest, exudes an air of mystique. The volcanic soil nurtures a flourishing ecosystem, creating a haven for diverse flora and fauna found nowhere else.

Ometepe Island holds a special place in Nicaraguan history, as it was once home to indigenous communities dating back thousands of years. The island's name, "Ometepe," derives from the Nahuatl language, meaning "Two Mountains." These ancient inhabitants left behind a wealth of archaeological treasures that continue to captivate visitors.

One of the notable sites on Ometepe Island is the town of Altagracia, located on the southeastern side. Here, you can explore the San Juan Bautista Church, an architectural gem that stands as a testament to the island's cultural significance. As you step inside, you'll encounter a unique fusion of Catholicism and indigenous beliefs. Adorning the walls of the church are ancient pre-Columbian stone statues known as "petroglyphs." These intricate carvings depict various symbols and figures, offering glimpses into the spiritual practices of the indigenous peoples who once called this island home.

The petroglyphs found within the San Juan Bautista Church are believed to have served as sacred markers, representing a connection between the physical and spiritual realms. They are a testament to the island's indigenous heritage and a reminder of the profound reverence early inhabitants held for the natural world. Exploring these petroglyphs provides a rare opportunity to delve into the island's past and gain insight into the beliefs and customs of its ancient inhabitants.

Beyond Altagracia, Ometepe Island beckons adventurers to explore its natural splendors. Hiking trails wind their way through lush forests, offering opportunities to witness the island's abundant wildlife. Colorful birds flit among the branches, while howler monkeys serenade visitors with their distinctive calls. The island's biodiversity extends to the surrounding waters, where you can engage in fishing or take a refreshing swim in the lake.

For those seeking a more adrenaline-fueled experience, hiking up one of the island's volcanoes is an unforgettable adventure. Concepción, the more challenging of the two, rewards intrepid climbers with breathtaking panoramic views from its summit. The journey to the top is a test of endurance and willpower, but the sense of achievement upon reaching the peak is immeasurable. Maderas, on the other hand, presents a gentler climb, taking you through verdant forests and leading to a tranquil crater lagoon at its summit.

As you traverse the island, you'll encounter small villages and welcoming communities, where the local residents proudly share their traditions and stories. Immerse yourself in the warmth and hospitality of the island's inhabitants, and you'll gain a deeper appreciation for the unique way of life on Ometepe.

To complete your exploration of Ometepe Island, take time to relax on its picturesque beaches. Playa Santo Domingo, with its soft sands and calm waters, offers an ideal spot to unwind and soak up the island's tranquility. Witness the vibrant colors of a sunset painting the sky as the sun sinks below the horizon, casting a golden glow upon the volcanoes and casting a spell of serenity over the entire island.

Ometepe Island is a destination that beckons nature lovers, adventure seekers, and history enthusiasts alike. Its extraordinary combination of awe-inspiring landscapes and archaeological marvels provides a unique and immersive experience. Whether you're hiking the volcanoes, discovering the ancient petroglyphs, or simply basking in the island's natural beauty, Ometepe will leave an indelible mark on your soul, drawing you back time and again to its enchanting shores.

San Juan del Sur: Coastal Charm and Pirate History

Nestled along Nicaragua's southwestern Pacific coast lies the charming town of San Juan del Sur, a hidden gem that has transformed from a quiet fishing village to a popular beach resort destination. With its breathtaking beaches, vibrant nightlife, and intriguing pirate legends, San Juan del Sur offers a captivating experience for travelers seeking sun, sand, and adventure.

Beaches of San Juan del Sur:

San Juan del Sur is renowned for its stunning beaches, where golden sands meet the crystal-clear waters of the Pacific Ocean. Whether you're a sun-worshipper, a surfer, or a nature enthusiast, the diverse array of beaches in and around San Juan del Sur will surely captivate you.

Playa San Juan del Sur:

Playa San Juan del Sur is the vibrant heart of the town, where locals and visitors alike gather to enjoy the sun, sand, and surf. Stretching along the scenic bay, this beach offers a picturesque setting that is perfect for a day of relaxation or beachside fun. The soft golden sands invite visitors to lay down their towels and bask in the warm Nicaraguan sun.

With the gentle waves of the Pacific Ocean rolling onto the shore, Playa San Juan del Sur is an excellent spot for swimming. The crystal-clear waters provide a refreshing escape from the heat, and the beach is generally safe for swimming. Families can enjoy building sandcastles or playing beach games, while couples can stroll hand in hand along the shoreline, taking in the breathtaking views.

The palm-fringed shoreline adds a tropical touch to the beach, providing shady spots to take a break from the sun's rays. Many beachfront restaurants and bars offer seating under the shade of palm trees, where visitors can enjoy a delicious meal or sip on a refreshing cocktail while taking in the panoramic views of the beach and bay. Whether you're craving local seafood specialties or international cuisine, the beachfront dining options cater to a variety of tastes.

Playa Maderas:

A short distance north of San Juan del Sur, Playa Maderas beckons surf enthusiasts from around the world. Renowned for its consistent waves and lively surf culture, this beach is a haven for both beginners and experienced surfers. The beach's consistent offshore winds create ideal conditions for surfing throughout the year.

Surf schools and board rentals are readily available at Playa Maderas, making it accessible for those eager to catch their first wave or improve their skills. Experienced instructors offer lessons for all levels, providing valuable guidance and ensuring a safe and enjoyable surfing experience. The friendly and supportive surf community adds to the welcoming atmosphere, making it a great place to connect with fellow surfers.

Beyond surfing, Playa Maderas offers a laid-back atmosphere where visitors can relax and soak up the beach vibes. The beach's natural beauty, with its rugged cliffs and golden sands, creates a picturesque backdrop for sunbathing or beachside yoga sessions. As the day draws to a close, don't miss the opportunity to witness the stunning sunset views from Playa Maderas, casting warm hues across the sky and painting a picture-perfect scene.

Playa Hermosa:

Located just a short drive from San Juan del Sur, Playa Hermosa lives up to its name, offering a truly beautiful and tranquil escape. This secluded beach is nestled amidst lush vegetation, providing a serene retreat away from the bustling town. Playa Hermosa's unspoiled beauty and calm waters make it an idyllic spot for those seeking a more peaceful and intimate beach experience.

Nature lovers will appreciate the pristine surroundings of Playa Hermosa. The beach is bordered by verdant hills and tropical forests, creating a natural paradise for birdwatching and wildlife spotting. The tranquil waters are perfect for swimming and snorkeling, allowing visitors to explore the underwater world filled with colorful marine life.

Playa Hermosa's tranquil ambiance and untouched landscape make it an ideal place to unwind and reconnect with nature. Visitors can find their own secluded spot along the beach, lay out a picnic blanket, and enjoy a picnic amidst the sounds of the crashing waves and the rustling of palm trees. Alternatively, hammocks swaying gently in the ocean breeze invite visitors to lounge and embrace the blissful tranquility.

Vibrant Nightlife and Dining Scene:

As the sun sets over San Juan del Sur, the town comes alive with its vibrant nightlife, offering a wide range of bars, clubs, and beachfront parties. From laid-back beach bars to lively clubs, there's something for every taste and mood.

Calle del Mar: A Culinary and Entertainment Haven

Calle del Mar, the pulsating main street running parallel to the beach in San Juan del Sur, is the epicenter of the town's vibrant nightlife and dining scene. This lively strip is a hub of activity, offering a diverse range of bars, restaurants, and entertainment venues that cater to every taste and preference.

Dining Delights:

As you stroll along Calle del Mar, tantalizing aromas waft through the air, enticing your taste buds with a multitude of culinary options. The street is lined with an array of restaurants, cafes, and eateries, offering a delightful fusion of local Nicaraguan dishes, international flavors, and delectable seafood creations.

Local Nicaraguan Cuisine:

Embrace the opportunity to sample traditional Nicaraguan specialties at the local restaurants dotting Calle del Mar. Indulge in the flavors of gallo pinto, the national dish made with rice and beans, accompanied by succulent grilled meats or fresh seafood caught straight from the nearby waters. Don't miss the chance to savor vigorón, a mouthwatering combination of yuca, cabbage, and pork rinds, served with a tangy tomato salsa.

Seafood Delicacies:

Given San Juan del Sur's coastal location, it comes as no surprise that the town boasts an abundance of fresh seafood options. From grilled lobster and shrimp ceviche to whole fried fish and ceviche mixto, the seafood restaurants along Calle del Mar offer an array of delectable dishes that highlight the region's culinary treasures from the sea.

International Flavors:

For those craving international cuisines, Calle del Mar does not disappoint. From Italian trattorias serving wood-fired pizzas and homemade pasta to trendy sushi bars offering fresh sushi rolls and sashimi, you can find a diverse range of international flavors to satisfy your cravings.

Vibrant Nightlife:

As the sun sets and darkness blankets San Juan del Sur, Calle del Mar transforms into a vibrant hub of entertainment, drawing locals and visitors alike to experience the town's legendary nightlife.

Bars and Lounges:

The lively strip is lined with a plethora of bars and lounges, each offering its unique ambiance and drink selection. From cozy beach bars with sand-covered floors and hammocks to trendy rooftop lounges boasting panoramic views of the bay, there's a venue to suit every mood and preference. Sip on handcrafted cocktails, savor local rum specialties, and mingle with fellow travelers as you soak up the vibrant atmosphere of San Juan del Sur's nightlife.

Occasional Live Music:

Calle del Mar occasionally comes alive with the sound of live music, adding an extra layer of entertainment to your night out. Local bands and musicians often perform at various venues along the street, showcasing the rich musical heritage of Nicaragua. From traditional folk music to contemporary tunes, the live music scene on Calle del Mar offers an immersive cultural experience.

Sunday Funday: A Legendary Pool Crawl

For a truly unique and unforgettable nightlife experience in San Juan del Sur, make sure to partake in the legendary Sunday Funday. This all-day event, held every Sunday, brings together locals and travelers alike for a day filled with poolside parties, games, and non-stop fun.

Sunday Funday kicks off at one designated pool, where participants gather to socialize, enjoy music, and indulge in refreshing drinks. As the day progresses, the event moves to different pools in the area, creating a dynamic and ever-changing party atmosphere. Along the way, you'll have the opportunity to engage in various poolside games and activities, meet new people, and create lasting memories.

The culmination of Sunday Funday is an epic beach party that takes place as the sun sets over the Pacific Ocean. Dancing barefoot in the sand, watching the vibrant colors of the sky, and reveling in the energetic atmosphere, you'll experience the true spirit of San Juan del Sur's nightlife.

Pirate Legends and History:

San Juan del Sur is not only a beach paradise but also a place rich in pirate legends and captivating history. The town's strategic location and its history as a trading port attracted famous pirates and privateers during the colonial era.

The Pirate Morgan: A Legacy of Adventure and Intrigue

San Juan del Sur carries a captivating pirate history, with one of the most legendary figures associated with the town being Captain Henry Morgan. Known for his daring exploits and cunning tactics, Morgan's presence in the region left an indelible mark on San Juan del Sur's identity and continues to intrigue visitors to this day.

According to folklore and historical accounts, Captain Henry Morgan used the sheltered bay of San Juan del Sur as a strategic hideout to plan his attacks on Spanish galleons, laden with treasures from the New World. The bay's natural geography, with its secluded coves and deep waters, provided the perfect setting for Morgan and his crew to lay in wait for unsuspecting ships. From his hidden base in San Juan del Sur, Morgan would launch surprise assaults, overwhelming and plundering the Spanish vessels, accumulating vast amounts of wealth.

The tales of Morgan's exploits have become woven into the fabric of San Juan del Sur's history and culture. Travelers visiting the town can delve into this fascinating pirate legacy through various pirate-themed tours and excursions. Expert guides regale visitors with stories of Morgan's daring escapades, recounting the battles fought, the treasures seized, and the daring escapes from the clutches of the Spanish authorities.

These immersive experiences allow visitors to explore the pirate's stomping grounds and gain insights into the strategies employed by Morgan and his crew. Tours may include visits to strategic lookout points, hidden caves rumored to have housed pirate treasures, and replicas of pirate ships, providing a glimpse into the adventurous world of Captain Henry Morgan.

The Ruins of Fortaleza La Polvora: A Window to the Town's Defensive Past

Perched majestically atop a hill overlooking San Juan del Sur, the ruins of Fortaleza La Polvora stand as a testament to the town's defensive past. Constructed in the 18th century, this fortress was built with the purpose of safeguarding San Juan del Sur from pirate attacks and protecting its valuable assets from plunder.

Fortaleza La Polvora, which translates to "Powder Fortress," derived its name from the ammunition and gunpowder stores that were once housed within its walls. The fort was strategically positioned to provide a vantage point over the bay, enabling its defenders to monitor and repel any pirate incursions.

Today, the ruins of Fortaleza La Polvora offer visitors a fascinating glimpse into the town's history and serve as a captivating historical site. Exploring the remnants of the fort allows you to envision the challenges faced by the early inhabitants of San Juan del Sur and appreciate the efforts made to protect the town and its inhabitants from pirate raids.

The panoramic views from the ruins are a highlight in themselves, providing sweeping vistas of the bay, the surrounding lush landscapes, and the vast expanse of the Pacific Ocean. Visitors can climb the weathered stone staircases and explore the remnants of the fortress walls, towers, and chambers, imagining the fort's former grandeur and the defensive strategies employed during its heyday.

As you stand amidst the ruins, you can almost sense the echoes of history, envisioning the town's defenders scanning the horizon for any signs of pirate ships and bracing themselves for potential attacks. The ruins of Fortaleza La Polvora are not only a testament to San Juan del Sur's defensive past but also a captivating destination for history enthusiasts and those seeking a deeper understanding of the town's heritage.

Beyond the Beaches:

While San Juan del Sur's beaches and nightlife steal the spotlight, there's more to explore in the surrounding area, offering opportunities for adventure and cultural immersion.

Nature and Wildlife:

San Juan del Sur is not only a haven for beach lovers but also a paradise for nature enthusiasts. From boat tours to hiking adventures, there are plenty of opportunities to explore the region's diverse flora and fauna.

Embark on a boat tour to discover the abundant marine life surrounding San Juan del Sur. Hop on a boat and venture into the ocean to spot playful dolphins as they swim alongside the vessel. You might even have the chance to witness the graceful beauty of sea turtles as they glide through the waves. The olive ridley sea turtles, in particular, make their way to the nearby La Flor Wildlife Refuge between July and January to nest on the sandy shores. Take part in a guided tour to observe this incredible natural phenomenon, where thousands of turtles lay their eggs and hatchlings make their way to the sea.

For those who prefer to explore on foot, nearby nature reserves offer fantastic hiking experiences. The Mombacho Volcano Nature Reserve beckons with its misty cloud forests and an extensive trail network. Lace up your hiking boots and venture into this lush paradise, where you'll encounter a rich variety of plant and animal species. Keep an eye out for howler monkeys swinging through the trees, vibrant orchids adorning the forest floor, and a plethora of colorful bird species flitting about. The reserve also offers the opportunity to hike up the volcano's slopes, rewarding you with breathtaking panoramic views of Lake Nicaragua and the surrounding landscape.

Another nature reserve worth exploring is the El Chocoyero-El Brujo Reserve. This hidden gem is renowned for its stunning waterfall and its resident population of Pacific green parakeets, locally known as "chocoyos." Embark on a guided hike through the reserve's trails, surrounded by dense foliage and the calming sound of rushing water. As you reach the waterfall, witness the mesmerizing sight of water cascading down the rocks into a serene pool below. If you're lucky, you may spot the vibrant green plumage of the chocoyos as they nest in the cliffs surrounding the waterfall.

Day Trips and Excursions:

San Juan del Sur serves as an ideal base for exploring the surrounding region, with a variety of day trips and excursions to nearby attractions that showcase the cultural and natural wonders of Nicaragua.

A short drive from San Juan del Sur is the picturesque town of Rivas. Stroll through its streets lined with colorful colonial buildings and visit the historic church, Iglesia de San Pedro. Explore the local market, where you can immerse yourself in the vibrant atmosphere and discover traditional handicrafts, fresh produce, and local delicacies. Rivas offers a glimpse into Nicaraguan daily life and is a great place to experience the country's authentic charm.

For a vibrant cultural experience, head to the colorful markets of Masaya. Known for its handicrafts, this bustling city is home to the famous Masaya Artisan Market. Browse through a wide array of traditional pottery, textiles, hammocks, and other locally crafted goods. Interact with artisans, observe their craftsmanship, and take home a piece of Nicaraguan artistry.

No visit to San Juan del Sur would be complete without a trip to the majestic Ometepe Island. Situated in Lake Nicaragua, this island is formed by two towering volcanoes, Concepción and Maderas. Take a ferry from San Jorge to Ometepe and explore the island's natural beauty. Hike through lush forests, swim in freshwater springs, or simply relax on the island's beautiful beaches. Discover ancient petroglyphs, visit coffee plantations, and immerse yourself in the island's rich cultural heritage.

San Juan del Sur offers a perfect blend of beach paradise, vibrant nightlife, and opportunities for adventure and exploration. Whether you're seeking relaxation, wildlife encounters, cultural immersion, or adrenaline-pumping activities, this enchanting town invites you to embrace its warmth and beauty. Indulge in the stunning coastline, immerse yourself in the wonders of nature, and create cherished memories that will last a lifetime.

By exploring these colonial cities and other historical sites in Nicaragua, you'll delve deep into the country's past, uncovering fascinating stories and immersing yourself in its rich cultural heritage.

Thrilling Activities and Adventure

Surfing and Water Sports

Nicaragua's Pacific coastline is renowned for its world-class surf breaks, attracting surfers from around the globe. With consistent swells, warm waters, and uncrowded beaches, Nicaragua offers an unforgettable surfing experience for beginners and seasoned wave riders alike. Here are some of the top surf spots to explore:

Playa Maderas: Located near San Juan del Sur, Playa Maderas is a picturesque beach that has gained popularity among surfers of all levels. This stunning stretch of coastline offers consistent waves throughout the year, making it a fantastic spot for both beginners and intermediate surfers. The sandy bottom and manageable wave sizes provide an ideal learning environment for those new to surfing. Aspiring surfers can take advantage of the surf schools and experienced instructors available on-site, who offer lessons tailored to individual skill levels and goals.

For more experienced surfers, Playa Maderas has additional breaks further out that offer a more challenging experience. These breaks provide larger and faster waves, perfect for riders seeking a bit more excitement and progression. The diversity of waves at Playa Maderas makes it an excellent destination for surfers looking to refine their skills or push their limits.

Popoyo: Situated in the Tola region, Popoyo is a world-renowned surf spot that attracts experienced surfers seeking powerful and hollow waves. The beach is known for its consistent swells and the quality of its surf breaks. Popoyo is particularly favored by thrill-seekers looking for fast barrels and challenging conditions.

One of the highlights of Popoyo is its versatility, offering both left and right-hand breaks. This diversity caters to surfers with different styles and preferences. Whether you're a regular-footed or goofy-footed surfer, you'll find waves to suit your stance. The adrenaline rush that comes from riding the powerful and hollow waves at Popoyo is truly unforgettable, making it a must-visit destination for advanced surfers seeking a memorable surfing experience.

Playa Colorado: Located within the Hacienda Iguana resort, Playa Colorado is renowned as a world-class surf break that lures experienced surfers from around the globe. This right-hand reef break is known for its long, powerful rides and the potential to produce some of the best waves in the country. The wave at Playa Colorado is often characterized by its barreling sections, providing the perfect canvas for experienced surfers to display their skills.

The wave at Playa Colorado demands respect and skill due to its fast and challenging nature. Intermediate and advanced surfers seeking epic barrels will find their paradise here. The surrounding natural beauty and the exclusive atmosphere of the Hacienda Iguana resort add to the overall allure of Playa Colorado, making it an extraordinary destination for surfers looking for a world-class wave and a unique experience.

Playa Hermosa: Just a short distance from San Juan del Sur, Playa Hermosa is a stunning beach that lives up to its name. It offers consistent waves that are suitable for surfers of all levels, making it an ideal spot for beginners and intermediate surfers. The sandy bottom break provides a forgiving environment for practicing maneuvers and honing surfing skills.

Playa Hermosa boasts both left and right-hand waves, ensuring that surfers can enjoy their preferred stance. The beauty of Playa Hermosa lies not only in its surf conditions but also in its natural surroundings. Pristine stretches of sandy beach, lined with palm trees and untouched tropical landscapes, create a serene atmosphere that enhances the surfing experience.

Whether you're a novice surfer looking to catch your first wave or an intermediate rider seeking a laid-back and scenic surf spot, Playa Hermosa offers the perfect blend of waves, beauty, and accessibility.

Best Seasons and Conditions for Surfing

Nicaragua's surf season generally runs from April to October, coinciding with the rainy season when the swells are most consistent. During this period, the southern and central Pacific coastlines receive larger swells, providing excellent conditions for surfers. The average water temperature hovers around a pleasant 80°F (27°C) year-round, so a wetsuit is often unnecessary.

It's important to note that Nicaragua can experience offshore winds in the morning, creating clean and groomed waves. As the day progresses, onshore winds may pick up, resulting in choppier conditions. Therefore, early morning surf sessions are recommended for optimal wave quality.

Surf Schools and Lessons for Beginners

For those eager to learn how to surf or improve their skills, Nicaragua offers numerous surf schools and experienced instructors ready to assist. These schools provide a safe and supportive environment for beginners, with lessons tailored to individual needs. Here's what you can expect from surf schools in Nicaragua:

Qualified Instructors: Surf schools in Nicaragua employ experienced instructors who are passionate about teaching and dedicated to ensuring a positive learning experience for students.

Equipment Rental: Surf schools typically provide surfboards and other necessary equipment, such as leashes and wax. They will guide you in selecting the appropriate board based on your skill level and the wave conditions.

Beginner-Friendly Beaches: Surf schools often choose beginner-friendly beaches with mellow waves and sandy bottoms, ensuring a safe and comfortable learning environment.

Step-by-Step Instruction: Surf lessons usually begin with a brief introduction to surfing fundamentals, including proper paddling techniques, board control, and how to catch and ride a wave. Instructors will provide hands-on guidance and feedback to help you progress quickly.

Safety Guidelines: Surf schools prioritize safety and will educate beginners on essential safety measures, such as how to navigate the lineup, avoid collisions, and handle wipeouts. They will also provide information on ocean currents, tides, and potential hazards specific to each surf spot.

Surfing Etiquette and Safety Tips

Respecting the ocean and fellow surfers is crucial to ensure a harmonious and enjoyable surfing experience. Here are some key surfing etiquette and safety tips to keep in mind:

Know the Right of Way: Understand the rules of priority in the lineup. Typically, the surfer closest to the peak has the right of way. Yielding the right of way prevents collisions and maintains order in the lineup.

Paddle Wide: When paddling back out after catching a wave, paddle wide around the breaking waves to avoid interfering with other surfers' rides.

Communicate and Be Aware: Maintain clear communication with fellow surfers, signaling your intentions and awareness of your surroundings. Pay attention to other surfers' positions to avoid collisions.

Respect Local Surfers: Show respect for the local surfing community. Observe and learn from experienced locals, follow local rules, and be mindful of any local customs or sensitivities.

Take Care of the Environment: Preserve the pristine beauty of Nicaragua's beaches by picking up trash, avoiding damage to coral reefs or other fragile ecosystems, and respecting wildlife habitats.

Beyond Surfing: Other Water Sports in Nicaragua

While Nicaragua is renowned for its surfing opportunities, the country also offers a variety of other thrilling water sports for adventure enthusiasts. Here are some exciting alternatives to surfing:

Stand-up Paddleboarding (SUP): Stand-up paddleboarding, often referred to as SUP, has become increasingly popular worldwide, and Nicaragua's diverse waterways offer the perfect setting for this enjoyable activity. With calm bays, estuaries, and lakes, SUP enthusiasts can glide across the water's surface while immersing themselves in Nicaragua's stunning scenery and abundant wildlife.

Picture yourself standing on a stable paddleboard, effortlessly propelling yourself forward with a paddle in hand. As you navigate Nicaragua's tranquil waters, you'll have the opportunity to spot a variety of wildlife. Keep your eyes peeled for colorful tropical birds perched on the shoreline or gracefully gliding above the water. Along the coastline, you may even come across curious dolphins or sea turtles, adding an element of wonder to your SUP adventure.

Kayaking and Canoeing: Nicaragua's vast waterways, such as the iconic Lake Nicaragua and the meandering San Juan River, beckon kayakers and canoe enthusiasts to explore their hidden treasures. Embark on a kayaking or canoeing journey and embark on an unforgettable expedition through Nicaragua's diverse ecosystems.

As you navigate the gentle currents, you'll find yourself immersed in the tranquility of nature. Paddle through mangrove forests, where the dense foliage creates a captivating backdrop and provides sanctuary for various bird species. Keep an eye out for herons, egrets, kingfishers, and even elusive species like the jabiru stork. Discover hidden lagoons teeming with life, where you can take a break from paddling and embrace the serenity of these secluded oases.

Jet Skiing and Wakeboarding: For those seeking a dose of adrenaline and high-speed excitement on the water, Nicaragua offers jet skiing and wakeboarding experiences that will leave you exhilarated. At popular coastal destinations, you'll find rental services that provide jet skis and equipment, allowing you to zip across the waves and feel the wind in your hair.

Whether you're a seasoned pro or a first-time rider, expert instructors are available to guide you through the basics and ensure a safe and thrilling experience. Feel the rush of acceleration as you navigate the waves, carving through the water with agility and precision. For those with a knack for wakeboarding, strap on your board and ride the wake created by a motorboat, performing impressive tricks and jumps.

Kiteboarding and Windsurfing: Nicaragua's steady coastal winds make it an ideal destination for kiteboarding and windsurfing enthusiasts. The expansive beaches of Lake Nicaragua, particularly in the Tola region, provide the perfect playground for these exhilarating water sports.

Harness the power of the wind as you soar across the water's surface, propelled by a kite or a windsurfing sail. Experience the thrill of catching air and performing daring maneuvers. The warm waters and consistent winds create an inviting environment for riders of all levels, from beginners looking to master the basics to advanced riders seeking to push their limits.

Immerse yourself in the thrill of kiteboarding and windsurfing in Nicaragua, where the combination of natural beauty and favorable wind conditions will undoubtedly create unforgettable memories.

Whether you choose to ride the waves as a surfer or explore other water sports, Nicaragua's coastal and inland waters provide a playground for adventure seekers. Embrace the excitement, immerse yourself in the natural beauty, and create unforgettable memories in this Central American paradise.

Volcano Hiking and Trekking

Nicaragua is a land of fiery giants, boasting a remarkable collection of volcanoes that captivate the adventurous souls seeking thrilling experiences and breathtaking natural wonders. Situated along the Pacific Ring of Fire, this Central American country is home to numerous active, dormant, and extinct volcanoes, each with its own unique characteristics and allure.

Notable Volcanoes and Their Characteristics:

Volcán Masaya: Witnessing the Active Crater

One of the most accessible and renowned volcanoes in Nicaragua is Volcán Masaya, a true natural wonder located just a short distance from the bustling capital city of Managua. Nestled within the Masaya Volcano National Park, this active volcano offers visitors a chance to witness the raw power of nature up close. Its active crater, Santiago, is a sight to behold, emitting a dramatic plume of smoke and occasionally spewing molten lava into the air.

Visitors have the unique opportunity to drive up to the rim of Volcán Masaya, where they can witness the awe-inspiring spectacle firsthand. As you approach the crater, the air thickens with a distinctive scent of sulfur, reminding you of the volcano's formidable nature. From the observation point, you can gaze into the depths of the active crater, marveling at the intense energy and forces at work beneath the Earth's surface.

Apart from the mesmerizing view from the rim, Masaya Volcano National Park offers walking trails that allow you to explore the volcanic landscape and delve deeper into the fascinating geology and history of the area. The trails wind through rocky terrain, revealing ancient lava fields and remnants of past eruptions. Along the way, you may encounter hardy plants that have adapted to survive in the harsh volcanic environment.

As you explore the park, keep an eye out for wildlife that has made its home in this unique ecosystem. Birdwatchers will delight in spotting various avian species, including parakeets, owls, and the colorful Montezuma oropendola. Lizards, bats, and other small creatures also inhabit the park, adding to the biodiversity that thrives amidst the volcanic surroundings.

Volcán Mombacho: A Cloud Forest Adventure

Located near the colonial city of Granada, Volcán Mombacho offers a different kind of volcanic experience. This dormant stratovolcano is renowned for its lush cloud forest ecosystem, which teems with life and offers a tranquil escape from the bustling city below.

Ascending Volcán Mombacho involves navigating its winding roads that snake their way up the mountainside. As you ascend, you'll find yourself surrounded by dense vegetation, including towering trees, vibrant orchids, and dangling epiphytes. The air becomes cooler and crisper, a refreshing respite from the tropical heat below.

Upon reaching the summit, you'll be greeted by an enchanting world of mist and greenery. Nature trails lead you through the cloud forest, providing an opportunity to immerse yourself in the captivating ecosystem. Along the way, you'll encounter an abundance of flora, such as bromeliads, ferns, and mosses, adding an ethereal touch to the surroundings.

Keep your eyes peeled for the myriad bird species that call Mombacho home. The volcano is a birdwatcher's paradise, with sightings of resplendent quetzals, emerald toucanets, and the endemic Mombacho hummingbird. Monkey troops may also make an appearance, swinging through the treetops and adding a playful charm to your journey.

At the viewpoints scattered across the summit, prepare to be awed by the breathtaking panoramic views that stretch as far as the eye can see. From this vantage point, you can admire the colonial city of Granada nestled by the shores of Lake Nicaragua, as well as the surrounding landscapes of verdant forests and neighboring volcanoes.

Volcán Concepción: Challenging Ascent on Ometepe Island

Rising majestically from the middle of Lake Nicaragua, Ometepe Island is a haven for nature lovers and adventure seekers. At its heart lies Volcán Concepción, an active stratovolcano that offers a challenging ascent for those seeking a thrilling and physically demanding adventure.

Embarking on the hike up Volcán Concepción is not for the faint of heart. The trail takes you through rugged terrain, dense forests, and steep slopes that will test your physical stamina and determination. As you make your way up, you'll be rewarded with stunning views of the island, the crystal-blue waters of Lake Nicaragua, and the neighboring volcano, Maderas.

The ascent is a true test of endurance, but the sense of accomplishment upon reaching the summit is unparalleled. Standing atop Volcán Concepción, you'll feel a profound connection with the raw power of nature. The panoramic vistas that unfold before your eyes are awe-inspiring, with sweeping views of the expansive lake and the lush landscapes of Ometepe Island.

While the challenging hike demands physical fitness and mental resilience, it is important to prioritize safety and adhere to the guidance of experienced guides or local authorities. Due to its active nature, Volcán Concepción may have restrictions or closures in place depending on the volcanic activity. Therefore, it is essential to stay informed and plan your ascent accordingly.

Telica Volcano: Nighttime Lava Views

For a truly unforgettable volcanic experience, Telica Volcano is a must-visit destination. Located in northwestern Nicaragua, Telica is known for its active lava lake and the rare opportunity to witness fiery displays at night.

The hike to Telica's summit takes you through a landscape of rugged trails and rocky landscapes, presenting a stark contrast against the surrounding lush greenery. As you ascend, the anticipation builds, knowing that you're on the verge of an extraordinary encounter with nature's raw power.

As darkness falls, a surreal transformation occurs. The red-hot lava within Telica's crater illuminates the night sky, casting an eerie glow that paints the surrounding landscape in shades of fiery orange. The crackling sounds of molten lava add to the ambiance, creating a truly mesmerizing experience that evokes a sense of both wonder and respect for the Earth's geological forces.

Sitting on the rim of Telica, you can observe the mesmerizing dance of molten lava below. The heat radiates from the depths, warming your skin and reminding you of the intense energy contained within the volcano. The starry night sky overhead provides a breathtaking backdrop as you witness this surreal encounter with nature's elements.

It's important to note that visiting Telica Volcano at night requires caution and preparation. Engaging the services of experienced local guides is highly recommended to ensure your safety and enhance your overall experience. They possess valuable knowledge of the terrain, local conditions, and safety protocols, allowing you to make the most of this extraordinary journey into the heart of a volcanic marvel.

Safety Guidelines for Volcano Hiking:

While volcano hiking in Nicaragua offers thrilling adventures, it's essential to prioritize safety. Here are some crucial guidelines to keep in mind:

Stay Informed: Before embarking on a volcano hike, gather up-to-date information about the volcano's activity, local regulations, and any potential risks. Consult with local authorities, park rangers, or experienced guides who have comprehensive knowledge of the volcano you plan to explore.

Choose the Right Season: Consider the best time of year for volcano hiking in terms of weather conditions and accessibility. Rainy seasons may increase the risk of landslides and hazardous trails, so plan your visit during the dry season for a safer experience.

Equip Yourself Properly: Wear sturdy, closed-toe hiking boots with good traction to navigate the often challenging terrains. Carry essential hiking gear, including a backpack with water, snacks, a first aid kit, a headlamp or flashlight, and a map or GPS device.

Hike with a Guide: Engaging the services of an experienced local guide is highly recommended, especially for challenging volcano hikes. They possess valuable knowledge about the terrain, weather patterns, and potential dangers. They can also enhance your experience by providing insights into the volcano's geology, history, and local folklore.

Respect Safety Perimeters: Some volcanoes may have restricted areas due to ongoing volcanic activity or potential hazards. Always abide by the safety perimeters set by park authorities and avoid venturing into prohibited zones. Remember that the safety of both yourself and the fragile ecosystems should be a top priority.

Conquering the Summit: Popular Volcano Hikes:

Embarking on the journey to conquer Nicaragua's volcanic summits is an extraordinary adventure that combines physical exertion, natural wonders, and a sense of triumph. Whether you seek close encounters with active craters or panoramic vistas from dormant volcanoes, these popular volcano hikes offer unforgettable experiences:

Volcán Masaya: Witnessing the Active Crater

The ascent to the rim of Volcán Masaya provides a unique opportunity to witness the active crater up close, offering an unforgettable experience for visitors of all skill levels. This relatively easy hike, suitable for both beginners and experienced hikers, takes you through a diverse landscape of volcanic terrain and leads you to the mesmerizing Santiago crater.

As you start your hike, you'll be greeted by the sights and sounds of the surrounding nature. The trail winds through lush vegetation, with occasional glimpses of wildlife and colorful bird species. The air is filled with the earthy scent of the volcano, heightening your anticipation for the grand spectacle that awaits.

As you approach the rim of the volcano, the intensity of the experience grows. The fuming Santiago crater emerges before your eyes, releasing plumes of smoke and occasionally displaying the fiery glow of molten lava. The raw power and energy of the volcano become palpable, creating a sense of awe and reverence.

Standing at the edge of the crater, you can feel the warmth and hear the gentle rumblings from deep within the Earth. The panoramic view from this vantage point offers a glimpse into the geological wonders of Nicaragua, with sweeping vistas of the surrounding landscape stretching as far as the eye can see.

Take your time to absorb the incredible scene before you. Observe the ever-changing nature of the plumes, the interplay of light and shadow, and the rugged beauty of the volcanic landscape. It's a moment that will be forever etched in your memory, a testament to the power and majesty of nature.

Volcán Mombacho: A Cloud Forest Adventure

Hiking through the cloud forest trails of Volcán Mombacho is an immersive experience that transports you to a world of enchantment and natural beauty. This dormant volcano, located near Granada, is a haven for nature enthusiasts and adventurers seeking to explore its lush vegetation, diverse wildlife, and captivating vistas.

As you embark on the hike, the scent of damp earth and the melodic chirping of birds fill the air. The trail meanders through dense cloud forest, where towering trees draped in epiphytes and orchids create a magical ambiance. Sunlight filters through the canopy, casting ethereal rays of light on the forest floor.

The diverse flora and fauna of Volcán Mombacho never fail to impress. Keep an eye out for howler monkeys swinging from tree branches, sloths lazily clinging to branches, and a plethora of bird species, including toucans and hummingbirds. The forest teems with life, offering endless opportunities for wildlife spotting and birdwatching.

As you ascend higher, the vistas become more expansive. At the summit, you are rewarded with panoramic views of Granada, Lake Nicaragua, and the surrounding landscapes. The sight of the tranquil lake juxtaposed against the verdant forest and distant volcanoes is a sight to behold.

Take a moment to soak in the serenity and tranquility of the summit. Enjoy a picnic amidst the cool mountain air, surrounded by nature's symphony. The experience of hiking through Volcán Mombacho's cloud forest is a true immersion into the wonders of the natural world, leaving you with a profound appreciation for Nicaragua's biodiversity.

Volcán Concepción: Challenging Ascent on Ometepe Island

Climbing Volcán Concepción on Ometepe Island is a physically demanding endeavor that rewards hikers with awe-inspiring panoramic views and a profound sense of accomplishment. This active stratovolcano, rising majestically from the middle of Lake Nicaragua, presents a challenging ascent that tests your endurance and determination.

The journey to the summit of Volcán Concepción begins with an early start, as the best time to hike is in the cool morning hours. As you make your way through the initial stages of the hike, you'll traverse rugged terrain and dense forests, encountering a diverse array of flora and fauna along the way.

The trail gradually becomes steeper, demanding increased physical exertion and mental focus. You'll navigate through rocky slopes, slippery terrain, and volcanic ash, requiring careful footwork and steady progress. The ascent is a test of your endurance, challenging you both physically and mentally.

As you ascend, the surrounding landscapes unfold in breathtaking fashion. Sweeping vistas of Lake Nicaragua, neighboring Volcán Maderas, and the verdant island of Ometepe reward your perseverance. The sense of achievement intensifies with each step, knowing that you're conquering the formidable heights of this active volcano.

Reaching the summit of Volcán Concepción is an extraordinary feat. Standing at the peak, you are rewarded with unobstructed views that stretch as far as the eye can see. The panoramic expanse showcases the beauty and grandeur of Ometepe Island, with its lush forests, fertile farmlands, and the vast expanse of the lake.

Surveying the surroundings from this vantage point, a profound sense of accomplishment and reverence washes over you. You have overcome the challenges of the ascent, experienced the power of nature firsthand, and witnessed the unparalleled beauty that Nicaragua has to offer.

Telica Volcano: A Nighttime Lava Adventure

Venturing into the darkness and witnessing the fiery spectacle of Telica Volcano at night is an otherworldly experience that leaves an indelible mark on your memory. The hike to Telica's summit offers a unique opportunity to observe the mesmerizing display of a lava lake, creating an atmosphere of mystery and awe.

As dusk falls, you begin your ascent, guided by the soft glow of headlamps and the anticipation of the fiery show ahead. The trail winds its way through the volcanic landscape, leading you closer to the heart of Telica. The starry sky above provides a celestial backdrop to the adventure unfolding.

As you approach the summit, the intensity of the experience grows. The air becomes charged with excitement as you catch glimpses of the glowing lava through the darkness. The deep red hues dance and flicker, casting an otherworldly glow on the surrounding rocks and creating an ethereal ambiance.

Reaching the rim of Telica Volcano, you settle into a vantage point that allows you to witness the mesmerizing display up close. The lava lake churns and spits, sending fiery sparks into the night sky. The sound of crackling lava and the rumbling of the volcano create an immersive sensory experience that evokes a sense of wonder and reverence.

As you sit in silence, absorbing the scene before you, time seems to stand still. The raw power and energy of the volcano become palpable, filling you with a profound appreciation for the forces that shape our planet. It's an encounter with nature's grandeur that few are privileged to witness, an experience that will forever be etched in your mind.

As the night draws to a close, you make your descent, carrying with you the memories of the extraordinary adventure you've just undertaken. The hike to Telica Volcano's summit at night offers a rare glimpse into the dynamic and awe-inspiring nature of volcanic activity, leaving you with a deep sense of respect for the forces that shape our world.

Note: Remember to always prioritize safety when venturing onto volcanoes. Stay informed about current volcanic activity, follow the guidance of experienced guides, and adhere to any safety regulations or recommendations provided by local authorities.

Immersing yourself in Nicaragua's volcanic landscapes is an adventure that unveils the raw power of nature while allowing you to push your limits and connect with the awe-inspiring forces that shape our planet. With proper preparation, respect for safety guidelines, and a sense of adventure, exploring Nicaragua's volcanoes will undoubtedly be an unforgettable highlight of your journey.

Canopy Tours and Zip-Lining

Nicaragua is a country blessed with lush rainforests, dense jungles, and diverse ecosystems, making it an ideal destination for adrenaline junkies and nature lovers. One of the most exhilarating ways to explore the country's natural beauty is through canopy tours and zip-lining. Canopy tours offer a unique opportunity to glide through the treetops, witnessing stunning panoramic views, and immersing yourself in the rich biodiversity of Nicaragua.

Safety Precautions and Equipment:

Safety is of paramount importance when embarking on canopy tours and zip-lining adventures in Nicaragua. These thrilling activities can provide an exhilarating experience, but it is crucial to prioritize safety to ensure a secure and enjoyable adventure. Here are some key considerations to keep in mind:

Operator's Safety Guidelines:

Before booking a canopy tour or zip-lining adventure, research and select reputable operators who prioritize safety. It is essential to ensure that the operators follow strict safety protocols and adhere to industry standards. Look for reviews and recommendations from previous participants to gauge the operator's commitment to safety.

Equipment Maintenance:

Ensure that the operator maintains their equipment properly. The use of high-quality harnesses, helmets, and other safety gear is vital for your protection. Check if the equipment is regularly inspected, well-maintained, and up to date. Faulty equipment can compromise your safety, so it is crucial to choose operators who invest in reliable gear.

Professional Guides:

Experienced and knowledgeable guides play a crucial role in ensuring your safety during canopy tours and zip-lining adventures. Look for operators who employ professional guides with extensive training in safety procedures, emergency protocols, and first aid. These guides should be well-versed in the specific challenges and nuances of the tour and able to provide clear instructions and guidance throughout the experience.

Participant Briefing:

A comprehensive participant briefing should be provided before the tour begins. This briefing typically covers safety guidelines, proper usage of equipment, and specific instructions for each activity. Pay close attention to these instructions and ask any questions you may have to ensure a clear understanding of what to expect and how to stay safe.

Weight and Health Restrictions:

Canopy tours and zip-lining adventures may have weight and health restrictions due to safety considerations. It is essential to disclose any relevant health conditions or physical limitations to the operator before participating. This information allows the operator to provide appropriate guidance and ensure your safety throughout the tour.

Emergency Preparedness:

Reputable operators should have established emergency protocols in place. Inquire about their emergency response procedures and ensure they have measures to address potential risks and handle unforeseen circumstances. Operators should also have a communication system in place to stay connected with their guides and participants throughout the tour.

Personal Responsibility:

While operators have a responsibility to provide a safe environment, it is also essential for participants to take personal responsibility for their safety. Follow the instructions given by the guides, use the provided safety gear correctly, and be mindful of your surroundings. Avoid engaging in reckless behavior that could compromise your safety or the safety of others.

Canopy Tour Options in Different Regions of Nicaragua:

something to suit every adventurer's taste. From rainforests to coffee plantations and enchanting cloud forests, the country showcases its natural wonders through a diverse range of experiences.

For those seeking the immersive beauty of the rainforest, Nicaragua's canopy tours provide an opportunity to delve deep into the lush foliage and experience the vibrant biodiversity up close. As you zip-line through the verdant canopy, you'll be surrounded by towering trees, the symphony of chirping birds, and the occasional glimpse of exotic wildlife. The rainforest canopy tours allow you to appreciate the intricate ecosystem and witness the harmonious coexistence of countless plant and animal species.

If you prefer a unique ambiance combined with adventure, a canopy tour in a coffee plantation might be the perfect fit. Nicaragua is renowned for its exceptional coffee, and some canopy tours take you soaring above the very plantations where this world-class coffee is grown. As you glide through the air, you'll be treated to panoramic views of rolling hills covered in coffee bushes, shaded by tall trees. The combination of adrenaline and the aroma of freshly roasted coffee creates an unforgettable sensory experience.

For those enchanted by misty landscapes and ethereal surroundings, a canopy tour in a cloud forest is sure to captivate your imagination. Nicaragua's cloud forests, nestled high in the mountains, offer a mystical atmosphere where mist swirls through the canopy, creating an otherworldly ambiance. Zip-lining through these enchanting forests allows you to feel a sense of serenity and tranquility as you glide silently above the fog-covered treetops. The cloud forest canopy tours provide an opportunity to witness unique plant species, spot rare birds, and immerse yourself in the captivating beauty of these elevated ecosystems.

No matter which region you choose to explore in Nicaragua, there is a canopy tour waiting to showcase the country's natural wonders. Whether you're seeking the raw and untamed beauty of the rainforest, the harmony between agriculture and nature in a coffee plantation, or the mystical allure of a cloud forest, Nicaragua's canopy tours provide an incredible opportunity to connect with nature and experience the thrill of soaring through the treetops.

Each canopy tour is carefully designed to provide a unique experience, ensuring that every adventurer can find a tour that aligns with their preferences and desires. So, whether you are an adrenaline junkie, a nature enthusiast, or simply seeking a new perspective on Nicaragua's breathtaking landscapes, embarking on a canopy tour is an adventure that will leave you with lasting memories and a deep appreciation for the country's natural wonders.

Experiencing the Thrill: Best Canopy Tours in Nicaragua

Mombacho Canopy Tour: A Rainforest Aerial Adventure

Located just a short distance from the historic city of Granada, the Mombacho Canopy Tour offers an unforgettable journey through the dense rainforest of the Mombacho Volcano Natural Reserve. The adventure begins with an exhilarating ascent of the volcano in a 4x4 vehicle, gradually climbing higher and leaving the bustling city behind. As you reach the treetop platforms, a feeling of excitement and anticipation builds up.

Strapped into your harness and equipped with all the necessary safety gear, you prepare to launch yourself into the air, suspended by the zip-line. The first thrilling zip sends you soaring through the rainforest canopy, surrounded by the symphony of wildlife and the fragrance of tropical flowers. As you glide from one platform to another, you can't help but marvel at the breathtaking views that unfold before you.

The Mombacho Canopy Tour treats you to panoramic vistas of the surrounding landscape. You'll catch glimpses of the impressive volcanic crater, with its mysterious steam rising from the depths. The shimmering waters of Lake Nicaragua extend into the distance, and the scattered Isletas archipelago dots the surface. The juxtaposition of the volcanic terrain, lush greenery, and sparkling blue waters creates a captivating sight that is truly awe-inspiring.

But the Mombacho Canopy Tour is not just about the adrenaline rush and stunning views; it's also an opportunity to learn about the incredible biodiversity of the rainforest. Knowledgeable guides accompany you throughout the tour, sharing their insights into the local flora and fauna. They'll point out the unique plant species, such as orchids and bromeliads, that thrive in this ecosystem. Keep an eye out for colorful birds, monkeys swinging through the trees, and other fascinating creatures that call this rainforest home.

Selva Negra Canopy Tour: Zip-lining in a Coffee Plantation

Nestled amidst the mountains of Matagalpa, the Selva Negra Canopy Tour offers a one-of-a-kind experience that combines the thrill of zip-lining with the scenic beauty of a working coffee plantation. As you ascend to the treetop platforms, you're immediately struck by the expansive views of the lush vegetation below and the rolling hills of coffee fields stretching into the horizon.

With each zip-line, you soar above the verdant coffee plantation, marveling at the intricate web of shade trees that provide the perfect conditions for coffee cultivation. From this bird's-eye perspective, you gain a deeper appreciation for the sustainable farming practices and the harmony between agriculture and nature. The symphony of bird songs fills the air as you glide through the canopy, occasionally catching glimpses of colorful toucans and other tropical avian species.

The Selva Negra Canopy Tour offers a series of zip-lines of varying lengths, allowing you to soak in the breathtaking landscape from different perspectives. As you zip from one platform to another, you can't help but feel a sense of freedom and exhilaration, accompanied by the sweet scent of coffee wafting through the air.

After the adventure, you can indulge in a well-deserved break at Selva Negra's café, where you can savor a cup of freshly brewed organic coffee. Immerse yourself in the aroma and flavors while learning about the intricate process of coffee production. Discover the passion and dedication that goes into cultivating and harvesting the beans, as well as the sustainable practices that promote biodiversity and environmental conservation within the plantation.

Montecristo Canopy Tour: Exploring the Cloud Forest

Located in the northern region of Estelí, the Montecristo Canopy Tour offers a truly enchanting and mystical experience for nature enthusiasts. This tour takes you deep into the heart of the cloud forest, a place where mist-shrouded canopies, ethereal landscapes, and vibrant flora create a surreal atmosphere.

As you embark on the zip-line adventure, the foggy landscape wraps around you, creating an otherworldly ambiance. The zip-lines crisscross through the dense forest, offering glimpses of the unique biodiversity that thrives in this enchanting environment. Keep your eyes peeled for colorful orchids clinging to tree branches, bromeliads decorating the trunks, and moss-covered ferns carpeting the forest floor.

Gliding through the foggy air, you'll have the opportunity to spot exotic bird species that call this cloud forest home. The resounding calls of toucans and the flash of iridescent feathers serve as reminders of the incredible avian diversity that thrives in this misty paradise. The Montecristo Canopy Tour allows you to observe these magnificent creatures in their natural habitat, fostering a deep sense of connection and appreciation for the fragile ecosystems that sustain them.

While the adrenaline rush of zip-lining through the cloud forest is undeniably thrilling, the experience also offers a tranquil escape from the demands of daily life. The peacefulness that permeates the air, coupled with the natural beauty surrounding you, instills a sense of serenity and harmony. It's an opportunity to disconnect from the modern world and reconnect with the wonders of nature.

The Montecristo Canopy Tour is an immersive journey that allows you to experience the cloud forest's magic firsthand. From the mist-laden canopy to the captivating biodiversity, this adventure leaves an indelible mark on your soul and reminds you of the incredible power and beauty of nature.

Canopy tours and zip-lining in Nicaragua provide an extraordinary way to experience the country's natural wonders. From the thrill of soaring through the treetops to the awe-inspiring views of volcanoes, rainforests, and coffee plantations, these adventures offer a unique blend of adrenaline and immersion in nature. Whether you choose the Mombacho Canopy Tour, Selva Negra Canopy Tour, or Montecristo Canopy Tour, each experience promises memories that will last a lifetime. So, gear up, embrace the excitement, and prepare to be captivated by the beauty of Nicaragua's canopy tours.

Wildlife Safaris and Birdwatching

Nicaragua's Diverse Ecosystems and Habitats

Nicaragua is truly a nature lover's paradise, boasting a remarkable variety of ecosystems and habitats that make it a haven for biodiversity. Situated between the Caribbean Sea and the Pacific Ocean, Nicaragua's unique geographical location plays a significant role in shaping its diverse landscapes and fostering a rich tapestry of life.

The country's lush rainforests are a sight to behold, with towering trees, dense vegetation, and a symphony of wildlife. These tropical rainforests provide a home to an astonishing array of flora and fauna, including countless species of plants, insects, mammals, and birds. From the vibrant orchids and bromeliads that adorn the forest canopy to the elusive jaguars and howler monkeys that roam beneath, the rainforests of Nicaragua offer a glimpse into a world teeming with life.

Moving inland, Nicaragua showcases its cloud forests, found in higher elevations where moisture-laden air becomes trapped by the mountains. These mystical forests are shrouded in mist and harbor a unique range of species adapted to the cool, humid conditions. Moss-covered trees, ferns, and epiphytic plants create a magical atmosphere, while resplendent quetzals, hummingbirds, and other rare bird species flit through the misty air.

In contrast to the verdant rainforests, Nicaragua's dry forests thrive in arid regions where rainfall is limited. These resilient ecosystems are characterized by drought-tolerant trees and shrubs that have adapted to survive in harsh conditions. Dry forests are home to an array of wildlife, including armadillos, iguanas, and numerous bird species that have evolved to withstand the challenges of the arid landscape.

Wetlands and mangroves play a crucial role in Nicaragua's ecological tapestry. These waterlogged areas serve as nurseries for fish and provide vital habitats for a multitude of species. Mangrove forests, with their intricate root systems and brackish waters, support a diverse range of marine and terrestrial life. They act as a buffer against coastal erosion, protect against storm surges, and provide nesting grounds for waterbirds such as herons, egrets, and kingfishers.

Nicaragua's coastal areas are a treasure trove of biodiversity, where land meets sea in a harmonious blend of ecosystems. Pristine beaches, rocky shores, and coral reefs provide habitats for countless marine species, while coastal forests and dunes offer refuge for migratory birds and nesting sea turtles. Along the Pacific and Caribbean coasts, you'll find an abundance of marine life, including dolphins, sea turtles, and vibrant coral reefs teeming with colorful fish.

Each of these diverse ecosystems is interconnected, creating an intricate web of life in Nicaragua. The country's commitment to conservation has led to the establishment of numerous protected areas and nature reserves, ensuring the preservation of these precious habitats and the species that call them home. By exploring Nicaragua's ecosystems, nature enthusiasts and wildlife lovers can witness firsthand the breathtaking beauty and incredible biodiversity that make this country a true gem of Central America.

Highlights of Wildlife Species and Birdlife

Nicaragua's rich biodiversity is a testament to the country's stunning natural landscapes and varied ecosystems. From dense rainforests to pristine rivers and lakes, Nicaragua is home to a plethora of wildlife species that will captivate nature enthusiasts and provide unforgettable wildlife safari experiences.

Venturing into the rainforests of Nicaragua offers the chance to encounter iconic mammals that inhabit these lush habitats. The elusive jaguars, with their striking coats and powerful presence, roam the dense undergrowth. Howler monkeys, known for their distinctive calls that echo through the trees, can be spotted swinging from branch to branch. Sloths, famous for their slow-paced lifestyle, lazily cling to tree branches, while ocelots, with their unique spotted patterns, stealthily traverse the forest floor. The rainforests are also home to tapirs, large herbivores known for their peculiar snouts, which can be spotted foraging near rivers and streams.

In addition to the impressive array of mammals, Nicaragua's rainforests are teeming with a remarkable variety of reptiles. The forests provide the perfect habitat for boa constrictors, one of the largest snake species in the country, which slither through the underbrush. Vibrant iguanas bask in the sun, displaying their colorful scales, while tree frogs add a touch of enchantment with their vibrant hues and melodious calls.

Nicaragua's rivers and lakes offer a different realm of wildlife, with a focus on freshwater species. Caimans, similar to alligators, can be found lurking in the waters, their eyes and snouts visible as they patiently wait for their prey. Turtles gracefully swim beneath the surface, occasionally surfacing to bask in the sun. Manatees, gentle giants of the water, glide through the rivers, their presence a true delight for lucky observers.

When it comes to birdwatching, Nicaragua is a haven with over 700 bird species to discover. The country's avian diversity is truly awe-inspiring, attracting birdwatchers from around the world. Both resident and migratory birds grace the skies, making Nicaragua a year-round destination for bird enthusiasts.

In the tropical forests, birdwatchers can spot an assortment of colorful and exotic species. Toucans, with their large and strikingly vibrant beaks, are among the most recognizable birds in Nicaragua. Parrots add bursts of color to the canopy, their squawks echoing through the trees. Hummingbirds, with their iridescent feathers and rapid wingbeats, hover around nectar-rich flowers. Trogon species, known for their beautiful plumage, can be observed perched on branches, while motmots display their unique tail feathers.

The wetlands and coastal areas of Nicaragua attract a multitude of water birds. Herons, with their long legs and elegant stature, wade through the shallow waters in search of fish. Egrets, with their delicate white plumage, grace the shores and marshes. Ibises, known for their distinctive curved bills, can be seen foraging in the mudflats. And the sight of flamingos, with their vibrant pink feathers, wading in the shallow lagoons is a true spectacle.

Nicaragua's rich biodiversity, impressive wildlife species, and abundant birdlife make it a premier destination for wildlife safaris and birdwatching. Whether exploring the rainforests, traversing the rivers, or observing the coastal areas, visitors will be rewarded with unforgettable encounters with rare and endangered species. The diversity of mammals, reptiles, and birds in Nicaragua showcases the country's commitment to conservation and offers a unique opportunity to appreciate the wonders of the natural world.

Immersing in the Wild: Wildlife Safaris and Reserves

To fully appreciate Nicaragua's incredible wildlife, embarking on wildlife safaris and visiting nature reserves is a must. Here are four exceptional destinations that offer unforgettable encounters with nature.

Indio Maíz Biological Reserve: Exploring the Rainforest

Located in southeastern Nicaragua, the Indio Maíz Biological Reserve is a sprawling protected area spanning approximately 4,500 square kilometers. It is nestled within the larger Mesoamerican Biological Corridor, recognized for its exceptional biodiversity and untouched natural beauty.

Stepping into Indio Maíz allows you to immerse yourself in one of Central America's most biologically diverse regions. The reserve is a sanctuary for a vast array of flora and fauna, including many rare and elusive species. The rainforest is home to majestic creatures such as jaguars, pumas, and harpy eagles, captivating visitors with their grace and beauty. As you traverse the reserve's network of trails, you'll encounter towering trees that form a dense canopy, allowing only shards of sunlight to filter through. The forest floor is adorned with vibrant orchids, bromeliads, and a rich tapestry of ferns, creating a stunning mosaic of colors and textures. The air is alive with the symphony of tropical birdcalls, as toucans, macaws, and hummingbirds flit from branch to branch. Spider monkeys swing effortlessly through the treetops, while sloths cling lazily to branches, seemingly in no hurry to move. Every step in Indio Maíz reveals a new wonder, and the experience of exploring this pristine rainforest is nothing short of awe-inspiring.

Juan Venado Island Nature Reserve: Mangrove Ecosystem

Situated along Nicaragua's Pacific coast, near the charming town of Las Peñitas, the Juan Venado Island Nature Reserve is a haven for mangrove forests and coastal biodiversity. This protected area stretches along a picturesque 22-kilometer-long coastline, encompassing mangrove swamps, estuaries, and sandy beaches.

Embarking on a boat or kayak excursion to explore Juan Venado Island allows you to witness the intricacies of the mangrove ecosystem up close. As you navigate the narrow waterways that wind through the mangroves, you'll be immersed in a world of serene beauty and remarkable biodiversity. Keep a keen eye out for both resident and migratory bird species that call this habitat home. Majestic frigatebirds soar gracefully overhead, while pelicans and herons elegantly stalk their prey in the shallow waters. The rhythmic calls of kingfishers reverberate through the air, adding to the tranquility of the surroundings. If you're lucky, you may even spot a nesting sea turtle or encounter the stealthy movement of a crocodile lurking in the mangrove channels. The waters teem with life as schools of fish dart beneath the surface, and crabs scuttle along the muddy banks. Rays glide effortlessly through the shallows, their wing-like fins creating a mesmerizing sight. Exploring Juan Venado Island offers a unique opportunity to appreciate the delicate balance of life within the mangrove ecosystem and witness the wonders of coastal biodiversity.

Maderas Volcano: Rainforest Trek and Wildlife Encounters

Situated on Ometepe Island within Lake Nicaragua, the Maderas Volcano provides an enthralling rainforest trekking experience. This dormant volcano stands proudly, reaching an elevation of 1,394 meters and is enveloped in lush vegetation, making it a hotspot for wildlife enthusiasts and adventurers alike.

Embarking on a trek through the dense rainforest of Maderas Volcano offers an opportunity to witness the wonders of nature at every turn. As you ascend, the melodious calls of birds fill the air. Vibrantly colored parrots and toucans gracefully glide above the canopy, their plumage creating a kaleidoscope of hues against the emerald backdrop. If luck is on your side, you may catch a glimpse of the resplendent quetzal, a bird revered for its radiant plumage and mythical significance. The rumbling echoes of howler monkeys reverberate through the trees, adding an otherworldly ambiance to the trek. Butterflies flutter by in a mesmerizing display of patterns and colors, adding a touch of enchantment to the rainforest experience. Occasionally, a white-faced capuchin monkey or a sloth can be spotted, reminding visitors of the rich diversity of wildlife that calls Maderas Volcano home. The trek offers not only physical challenges but also a chance to connect with the natural world, allowing one to appreciate the beauty and resilience of the rainforest ecosystem.

Estero Padre Ramos Nature Reserve: Birdwatching Paradise

Located along Nicaragua's Pacific coast, the Estero Padre Ramos Nature Reserve is a pristine wetland area renowned for its exceptional birdwatching opportunities. This coastal reserve encompasses lagoons, mangroves, and a variety of intertidal habitats, providing a rich feeding ground for numerous bird species.

Equipped with a pair of binoculars, traversing the trails and observation towers within the Estero Padre Ramos Nature Reserve offers an awe-inspiring avian spectacle. As you venture into the reserve, herons, egrets, spoonbills, and ibises gracefully wade through the shallow waters in search of fish and crustaceans. Their elegant movements and striking plumage create a captivating scene for bird enthusiasts. Above, ospreys and frigatebirds soar effortlessly, scanning the waters below for their next meal. The reserve's sandy shores provide a haven for an array of shorebirds, including sandpipers, plovers, and willets, as they scuttle along the shoreline, probing the sand for small creatures. The Estero Padre Ramos Nature Reserve is a haven for birdwatchers, where each moment presents an opportunity to witness the fascinating behaviors and vibrant colors of the avian inhabitants. Whether you're an avid birdwatcher or a casual observer, the reserve's diverse birdlife is sure to leave you in awe of nature's boundless beauty.

In conclusion, Nicaragua's wildlife safaris and birdwatching experiences offer an invitation to explore the country's diverse ecosystems and encounter its remarkable biodiversity. From the lush rainforests of Indio Maíz to the tranquil mangroves of Juan Venado Island, the captivating rainforest trek of Maderas Volcano, and the avian paradise of Estero Padre Ramos, each destination provides a unique opportunity to connect with nature and witness the wonders of Nicaragua's wildlife. These experiences leave visitors with a profound appreciation for the delicate balance of ecosystems and the need for their conservation, ensuring that future generations can continue to enjoy the splendor of Nicaragua's natural heritage.

Immersing in Nicaragua's Culture

Traditional Cuisine and Local Delicacies

Nicaraguan cuisine is a delightful fusion of indigenous, Spanish, and African influences, resulting in a diverse array of flavors and dishes that are sure to tantalize your taste buds. The country's rich agricultural resources, including rice, beans, corn, and tropical fruits, form the foundation of its traditional cuisine. Nicaraguan food reflects the country's history, geography, and cultural diversity, making it a truly unique and enjoyable culinary experience.

One iconic dish that you must try is gallo pinto, which is a staple breakfast dish in Nicaragua. It consists of rice and beans cooked together with onions, bell peppers, and spices. The combination of fluffy rice and tender beans creates a satisfying and flavorful base that is often accompanied by eggs, cheese, and plantains. Gallo pinto is not only delicious but also a cultural symbol representing Nicaraguan identity and national pride.

Vigorón is another popular dish that showcases the vibrant flavors of Nicaragua. It is a refreshing salad made with cabbage, tomatoes, and yuca (cassava), topped with crispy pork rinds. The tangy acidity of the cabbage, the earthy flavors of the yuca, and the savory crunch of the pork rinds create a harmonious blend of textures and tastes. This dish is commonly enjoyed as a light lunch or snack, especially during hot summer days.

When it comes to hearty and filling meals, nacatamal takes the spotlight. Nacatamal is a traditional dish that consists of steamed corn dough filled with a savory mixture of meat, vegetables, and spices. The filling typically includes pork, chicken, or beef, along with potatoes, onions, peppers, and olives. The dough is wrapped in a banana leaf and steamed until it becomes tender and fragrant. This labor-intensive dish is often prepared and enjoyed during special occasions and family gatherings, as it brings people together to savor its delicious flavors.

Indio viejo, meaning "old Indian," is a traditional stew that dates back to pre-Columbian times. It is made with ground corn, meat (such as beef or chicken), onions, garlic, tomatoes, bell peppers, and a variety of aromatic spices. The corn is ground into a fine meal, giving the stew a thick and hearty texture. Indio viejo is a comfort food that warms the soul, and its robust flavors and rich history make it a favorite among locals and visitors alike.

No exploration of Nicaraguan cuisine would be complete without mentioning the delightful local delicacies. Quesillo is a beloved treat that showcases the simplicity and elegance of Nicaraguan street food. It consists of a soft cheese called cuajada, which is wrapped in a warm tortilla and topped with onions, vinegar, and a hint of salt. The combination of the creamy cheese and tangy toppings creates a harmonious blend of flavors that is both satisfying and addictive.

For those seeking a hearty and flavorful meal, baho is a must-try dish. It is a traditional meat and vegetable stew that is slow-cooked to perfection. Baho typically includes cuts of beef or pork, plantains, yuca, and various vegetables. The ingredients are layered in a pot and cooked together, allowing the flavors to meld and create a deliciously savory dish. The tender meat, starchy yuca, and sweet plantains make each bite a delightful combination of textures and tastes.

If you're in the mood for something indulgent, fritanga is the answer. Fritanga is a platter of fried pork, beef, and plantains, often served with rice, beans, and cabbage salad. It is a popular street food option that offers a medley of flavors and textures. The crispy and flavorful meats, along with the sweet and savory plantains, create a mouthwatering combination that will satisfy your cravings and leave you wanting more.

Here are a few more traditional cuisine and local delicacies of Nicaragua:

Nica Tamales: Tamales are a popular dish in many Latin American countries, and Nicaragua has its own unique version called "Nica Tamales." These tamales are made with seasoned masa (corn dough) filled with meat (such as chicken or pork), vegetables, and sometimes even olives and raisins. The mixture is wrapped in banana leaves and steamed until cooked. Nica Tamales are often enjoyed during special occasions and holidays.

Rondón: Rondón is a traditional Afro-Caribbean dish that has made its way into Nicaraguan cuisine, particularly in the Caribbean coastal regions. It is a hearty seafood stew made with a variety of fish, shrimp, crab, coconut milk, yuca, plantains, and aromatic spices. The combination of fresh seafood and rich coconut flavors creates a delicious and comforting dish.

Rosquillas: Rosquillas are a type of traditional Nicaraguan biscuit or cookie. They are made with cornmeal, cheese (usually queso seco), butter, and sometimes flavored with anise or cinnamon. Rosquillas come in different shapes, ranging from round to twisted, and they have a satisfying crunch with a hint of saltiness from the cheese. These biscuits are enjoyed as a snack or dessert, and they pair well with a cup of coffee or hot chocolate.

Cacao-based Drinks: Nicaragua is known for its high-quality cacao, and cacao-based drinks are a specialty in the country. One popular drink is "Pinolillo," made from ground roasted corn, cacao powder, and spices. It is mixed with water or milk and sweetened with sugar. Pinolillo is a rich and slightly grainy beverage with a distinct chocolate flavor. Another traditional cacao-based drink is "Cacao de Bola," which is made by dissolving a cacao ball in hot water or milk. It creates a smooth and creamy chocolate drink that is often enjoyed during colder months.

Níspero: Níspero is a tropical fruit native to Nicaragua and is commonly referred to as the "Nicaraguan apricot." It has a vibrant orange color and a sweet, tangy flavor. Nísperos are typically eaten fresh, and they can be enjoyed on their own or used in various desserts, jams, and juices. Their unique taste and texture make them a favorite among locals and visitors alike.

Nicaraguan cuisine not only offers a delightful culinary experience but also provides a glimpse into the country's rich history and cultural heritage. The blending of indigenous, Spanish, and African influences has created a unique and diverse food culture that is worth exploring and celebrating. So, when you visit Nicaragua, be sure to indulge in these traditional dishes and local delicacies to truly immerse yourself in the flavors and traditions of this beautiful country.

Festivals and Celebrations

Nicaraguans take great pride in their vibrant and colorful festivals, which serve as a testament to their rich cultural heritage. These celebrations are a perfect opportunity for locals and visitors alike to immerse themselves in the lively traditions and experience the true essence of Nicaragua. From religious processions to joyful dances, the festivals of Nicaragua offer a captivating glimpse into the country's cultural tapestry.

Semana Santa, or Holy Week, stands out as one of the most renowned and widely celebrated festivals in Nicaragua. Taking place in various cities across the country, Semana Santa occurs during the week leading up to Easter Sunday. The festivities commence with Palm Sunday, where crowds gather to commemorate Jesus' entry into Jerusalem. Throughout the week, vivid processions wind their way through the streets, with participants dressed in elaborate costumes representing biblical figures. Carrying religious icons and crosses, the faithful engage in solemn rituals and prayers, creating a reverent atmosphere. The streets come alive with the sound of traditional music, including the enchanting notes of the marimba, adding to the spiritual ambiance. It is a time when Nicaraguans deeply connect with their faith and honor their religious traditions.

La Purísima, another significant religious festival, takes place in December, specifically on the eighth of the month, in honor of the Virgin Mary. This festival showcases Nicaragua's strong Catholic roots and is cherished by both young and old. Homes and churches are adorned with beautiful altars, intricately decorated with flowers, candles, and religious icons. Nicaraguan families open their doors to visitors, inviting them to participate in the festivities. Guests are welcomed with hymns dedicated to the Virgin Mary, and they join in singing traditional songs known as "Gozos." These songs express gratitude and devotion to the Virgin, celebrating her purity and grace. As a token of hospitality, hosts offer traditional sweets such as leche condensada (sweetened condensed milk) and drinks like chicha, a corn-based beverage. La Purísima is a time of unity and community, where people come together to celebrate their faith and show reverence for the Virgin Mary.

Palo de Mayo is another captivating festival deeply rooted in Nicaragua's African heritage. Celebrated primarily in the Caribbean coastal regions during the month of May, this vibrant event combines music, dance, and revelry. The festival originates from the Garifuna community, an Afro-indigenous group, and serves as a commemoration of their history and culture. The main highlight of Palo de Mayo is the Maypole dance, known as "baile de palo." Colorfully dressed dancers, accompanied by lively music featuring drums, marimbas, and other traditional instruments, gather around a tall, decorated pole. The dancers skillfully weave ribbons around the pole, creating intricate patterns as they move in synchronized steps. The energy is infectious, and spectators often find themselves joining the celebration, embracing the joyous spirit of the festival. Palo de Mayo is an extraordinary opportunity to experience the vibrant Afro-Caribbean culture of Nicaragua.

The Santo Domingo Festival, celebrated in the town of Managua, pays homage to Santo Domingo de Guzmán, the patron saint of the city. Held in August, this week-long event combines religious devotion with lively festivities. The festival kicks off with a colorful parade, where participants dress in traditional costumes and march through the streets. Traditional dances, such as the "Baile de Negras" (Dance of the Black Women) and the "Baile de Chinegro" (Dance of the Black and White), are performed with exuberance and skill. These dances reflect Nicaragua's multicultural heritage, incorporating African and indigenous influences. Throughout the festival, locals and visitors alike partake in various activities, including carnival rides, live music concerts, and street food stalls offering delicious Nicaraguan delicacies. The Santo Domingo Festival is a vibrant celebration that unites the community and showcases the rich cultural diversity of Nicaragua.

In addition to these major festivals, Nicaragua has a multitude of other cultural events and celebrations that take place throughout the year. For example, the May Pole Festival in Bluefields, the Feast of San Sebastián in Diriamba, and the August Carnival in Managua are just a few more occasions where locals come together to celebrate their cultural traditions.

Attending these festivals provides a unique opportunity to witness the passionate spirit of the Nicaraguan people and engage with their customs and rituals. It is a chance to embrace the warmth of the local community, partake in traditional dances, savor authentic cuisine, and immerse oneself in the vibrant music that fills the air. These festivals serve as a reminder of the deep-rooted cultural pride that Nicaraguans carry with them, and they welcome visitors to share in their joyful celebrations.

Here are a few more notable festivals and celebrations that showcase the vibrant spirit of Nicaragua:

Fiesta de Santo Domingo de Guzmán (Masaya): Held in the city of Masaya, this week-long festival honors Santo Domingo de Guzmán, the patron saint of the city. The festivities include lively processions, traditional dances, live music performances, and a grand fireworks display. Masaya is known for its vibrant arts and crafts scene, and during the festival, artisans showcase their skills and creations at the famous Masaya Craft Market.

Feria Agostina (León): Celebrated in the city of León during the month of August, Feria Agostina is a cultural extravaganza that combines art, music, dance, and culinary delights. The festival features parades, concerts, art exhibitions, traditional bullfights, and a wide array of food stalls offering local delicacies. It is a fantastic opportunity to experience the vibrant atmosphere of León and immerse oneself in Nicaraguan culture.

Festival de la Virgen de Candelaria (Solentiname Islands): Taking place in the picturesque Solentiname Islands in Lake Nicaragua, this festival pays homage to the Virgen de Candelaria. It features a unique blend of indigenous and Catholic traditions, with colorful processions, traditional dances, and spiritual ceremonies. The festival provides a glimpse into the cultural heritage of the indigenous communities that reside on the islands.

Carnaval de San Juan (San Juan del Sur): San Juan del Sur, a popular beach town on the Pacific coast, hosts the vibrant Carnaval de San Juan in late June. The festival celebrates the town's fishing and seafaring traditions. Colorfully decorated boats sail along the coastline, accompanied by music, dancing, and revelry. The streets come alive with parades, beach parties, and water-based activities, creating an electrifying atmosphere.

La Griteria (Granada and other cities): La Griteria, also known as the "Shout of Joy," is a religious festival celebrated on December 7th in various cities across Nicaragua. It commemorates the Immaculate Conception of the Virgin

Mary. During the festival, locals gather in churches and public squares, holding candles and singing hymns dedicated to the Virgin. The highlight of the celebration is the "Gritería," where people shout "¿Quién causa tanta alegría?" (Who causes so much joy?), and the crowd responds with "¡La Concepción de María!" (The Conception of Mary!). Traditional sweets and drinks are distributed during the festivities.

These festivals and celebrations provide a glimpse into the cultural richness of Nicaragua, allowing visitors to engage with local traditions, taste authentic cuisine, witness traditional dances, and experience the joyous spirit of the Nicaraguan people. Each festival has its own unique flair and significance, offering a memorable and immersive experience for travelers seeking to connect with the vibrant cultural fabric of Nicaragua.

Art and Craft Traditions

Nicaragua is a country that takes great pride in its vibrant and diverse artisan community. Throughout the country, you'll find talented craftsmen and women who dedicate themselves to preserving and showcasing Nicaragua's artistic traditions. From the bustling handicraft market in Masaya to the serene Solentiname Islands and the pottery town of San Juan de Oriente, each region offers its own unique artistic expressions.

The city of Masaya, located just south of the capital city Managua, is renowned for its handicraft market. Here, visitors are greeted with a kaleidoscope of colors and a bustling atmosphere as artisans proudly display their creations. Ceramics, woodwork, textiles, and leather goods fill the stalls, offering a glimpse into Nicaragua's rich artistic heritage. The ceramics, in particular, are a highlight, with intricate designs and vibrant glazes adorning each piece. Skilled craftsmen shape clay into various forms, from ornate vases and platters to delicate figurines. The techniques used in Masaya's ceramics have been passed down through generations, with each piece representing the skill and creativity of the artisans.

A visit to the Solentiname Islands in Lake Nicaragua offers a different artistic experience. These remote islands are home to a community of artists who have gained recognition for their vibrant paintings. Inspired by the natural beauty that surrounds them and the daily life of the region, the artists of Solentiname create works that reflect the essence of Nicaragua. The paintings often depict scenes of lush landscapes, wildlife, and everyday activities of the local people. The use of bold colors and intricate detailing brings these artworks to life, capturing the spirit and energy of the region. Visitors can explore the studios of the artists, witness their creative process, and even purchase original paintings as souvenirs.

In the town of San Juan de Oriente, located near Granada, pottery takes center stage. This small town has a rich history of pottery-making, and its artisans are highly regarded for their skill and craftsmanship. The techniques used in San Juan de Oriente have been passed down through generations, ensuring the preservation of traditional methods. Artisans work with clay, shaping it by hand or using a potter's wheel, to create exquisite vessels and sculptures. The designs are often inspired by nature, incorporating elements such as flowers, birds, and geometric patterns. Each piece is meticulously crafted, reflecting the passion and dedication of the artisans. Visitors to San Juan de Oriente can witness the pottery-making process, visit workshops, and even try their hand at creating their own pottery under the guidance of skilled artisans.

Beyond the individual regions, Nicaragua as a whole is known for its commitment to preserving cultural heritage. Artisan cooperatives and associations have been formed to support and promote traditional crafts. These organizations provide training, resources, and marketing opportunities for artisans, ensuring the continuity of their craft. Additionally, the government of Nicaragua recognizes the importance of the artisan sector and actively supports initiatives that promote cultural tourism and sustainable development.

Anecdotes and Examples:

One anecdote that highlights the talent and creativity of Nicaragua's artisans revolves around the famous hammocks of Masaya. Hammocks are an integral part of Nicaraguan culture, providing a comfortable and relaxing space for both rest and socializing. In Masaya, skilled artisans weave hammocks using traditional techniques passed down through generations. These hammocks are not just functional but also works of art. The intricate patterns, vibrant colors, and durable craftsmanship make them highly sought after by both locals and tourists. It is said that a well-made Nicaraguan hammock can last a lifetime, providing years of comfort and beauty.

In the Solentiname Islands, there is an inspiring story of how art has transformed the lives of the local community. The islands were once primarily inhabited by fishermen and farmers who faced economic challenges. In the 1960s, a priest named Ernesto Cardenal established an artistic community on the islands, encouraging the residents to express themselves through art. The community flourished, and the artists gained recognition both locally and internationally. Today, the art created on the Solentiname Islands has become a significant source of income for the community, helping to improve their quality of life and preserve their cultural heritage.

The pottery tradition in San Juan de Oriente also has its share of fascinating stories. One particular example is the legacy of the famous ceramic artist Juan Quezada, known for his innovative pottery techniques. Juan Quezada, from the neighboring country of Nicaragua, visited San Juan de Oriente in the 1970s and shared his knowledge and techniques with the local artisans. His guidance and mentorship sparked a revolution in the pottery community, introducing new methods and pushing the boundaries of traditional pottery-making. Today, the influence of Juan Quezada can still be seen in the intricate designs and exceptional quality of the pottery created in San Juan de Oriente.

In conclusion, Nicaragua's artisan community is a testament to the country's rich cultural heritage. From the bustling handicraft market of Masaya to the vibrant paintings of the Solentiname Islands and the exquisite pottery of San Juan de Oriente, Nicaragua offers a treasure trove of artistic expressions. Through their dedication and skill, the artisans of Nicaragua preserve traditions that have been passed down through generations, ensuring that the country's cultural heritage continues to thrive. Visitors to Nicaragua have the opportunity to immerse themselves in this world of creativity, witnessing the artistic process firsthand and taking home unique pieces that embody the spirit of Nicaragua.

Music and Dance of Nicaragua

Music and dance hold a special place in the heart of Nicaraguan culture, acting as a vibrant expression of joy, history, and social identity. They reflect the country's diverse heritage, blending indigenous, Spanish, and African influences into a tapestry of rhythmic melodies and captivating performances.

At the heart of traditional Nicaraguan music is the marimba, a wooden xylophone-like instrument. It is considered the national instrument of Nicaragua and is prominently featured in various genres of traditional music. The marimba consists of wooden bars, usually made from rosewood or cedar, that are struck with mallets to produce resonant tones. Its distinct sound resonates through the air, enchanting listeners and evoking a sense of nostalgia and cultural pride.

When it comes to traditional music, the marimba is often accompanied by guitars, drums, and other percussion instruments. These instruments form the backbone of the rich melodies that emanate from Nicaraguan gatherings and festivities. The rhythmic beats and intricate melodies create a lively atmosphere, inviting people to sway, dance, and immerse themselves in the vibrant energy.

One of the most celebrated traditional dances in Nicaragua is El Güegüense, a theatrical performance that dates back to colonial times. Recognized as a Masterpiece of the Oral and Intangible Heritage of Humanity by UNESCO, El Güegüense tells the story of a clever indigenous merchant who outwits Spanish colonial authorities through satire and humor. The performance combines music, dance, and spoken dialogue, creating a captivating spectacle that showcases the resilience and wit of the Nicaraguan people.

Another popular folk dance is El Palo de Mayo, which originated from the Afro-descendant communities on the Caribbean coast of Nicaragua. This lively dance is accompanied by infectious African-influenced music and features performers swaying and twirling around a decorated maypole. The vibrant rhythms and energetic movements of El Palo de Mayo reflect the spirit and resilience of the Afro-Nicaraguan community, and the dance has become a cherished symbol of their cultural heritage.

In addition to traditional music and dance, Nicaragua has also embraced contemporary genres such as salsa and merengue. These musical styles, with their lively beats and catchy melodies, have gained popularity and can be enjoyed in bars, clubs, and live performances in urban centers like Managua and Granada. Visitors have the opportunity to experience the vibrant nightlife and dance to the infectious rhythms of Nicaraguan salsa, creating unforgettable memories on the dance floor.

Anecdotes and personal experiences further illustrate the profound impact of music and dance on Nicaraguan culture. One such anecdote revolves around the marimba player Don Alberto Urroz. Born in Masaya, Don Alberto Urroz dedicated his life to mastering the marimba, becoming a revered figure in Nicaraguan music. His virtuosity and passion for the instrument captivated audiences both locally and internationally, leaving an indelible mark on the country's musical heritage.

Another anecdote relates to the annual Palo de Mayo Festival celebrated in Bluefields, a coastal city in eastern Nicaragua. During this festival, the streets come alive with vibrant music, pulsating rhythms, and the exuberant dance of Palo de Mayo. It is a time of unity and celebration, as people from all walks of life come together to honor their Afro-Nicaraguan roots and revel in the infectious energy of the dance.

Nicaraguan music and dance serve as cultural bridges, connecting generations and preserving ancestral traditions. They are not just forms of entertainment but also a way for Nicaraguans to connect with their roots, celebrate their history, and express their identity. Through the power of music and dance, Nicaraguans transmit their cultural heritage to younger generations, ensuring its longevity and fostering a sense of belonging and pride.

Practical Travel Tips

Transportation Options in Nicaragua

Transportation plays a crucial role in exploring Nicaragua's diverse landscapes and reaching various destinations within the country. Here are some transportation options to consider during your trip:

Domestic Flights:

Nicaragua's domestic flight network provides a convenient option for travelers looking to cover long distances quickly. The country has several domestic airports located in major cities and tourist destinations. Airlines such as La Costeña and Aerolineas Sosa operate regular flights connecting various regions within Nicaragua.

One of the primary advantages of domestic flights is the time saved on travel. For example, flying from Managua, the capital city, to the Corn Islands in the Caribbean can take less than two hours, whereas the journey by land and sea would require a significantly longer duration. Domestic flights are especially beneficial for travelers who have a limited time frame or wish to visit multiple destinations efficiently.

Additionally, flying within Nicaragua allows visitors to enjoy breathtaking aerial views of the country's diverse landscapes, including its lush rainforests, sparkling lakes, and dramatic volcanic formations. It is a unique experience that provides a different perspective on Nicaragua's natural beauty.

Public Buses:

Public buses are the backbone of transportation in Nicaragua and the most common mode of travel for both locals and budget-conscious travelers. They offer an affordable way to get around the country and connect major cities, towns, and even smaller rural communities.

Nicaragua's public bus system consists of various types of buses, ranging from large coach buses to smaller vans. They are often colorfully decorated and play lively music during the journey, creating a vibrant and lively atmosphere.

While public buses are a cost-effective option, it's important to note that they can be crowded, especially during peak hours and on popular routes. Be prepared for potential delays due to factors such as traffic, road conditions, and stops to pick up and drop off passengers along the way. Patience and flexibility are key when using public buses in Nicaragua.

One of the unique aspects of traveling by public bus in Nicaragua is the opportunity to interact with locals and experience the country's vibrant culture firsthand. Engaging in conversations with fellow passengers, hearing local stories and anecdotes, and observing the daily life of Nicaraguans can enrich your travel experience and provide valuable insights into the local way of life.

Private Shuttles:

For travelers seeking a more comfortable and convenient mode of transportation, private shuttles offer an excellent alternative. These shuttles provide door-to-door service, picking you up from your accommodation and taking you directly to your desired destination.

Private shuttles are particularly popular for traveling between popular tourist destinations, such as Granada, León, San Juan del Sur, and Ometepe Island. They are a hassle-free option, especially for those who prefer not to navigate public transportation or have limited time to spare.

Private shuttles can be arranged through tour operators, travel agencies, or even your accommodation. They offer flexibility in terms of departure times and routes, allowing you to tailor your travel itinerary according to your preferences. Additionally, private shuttles often come with knowledgeable drivers who can provide valuable insights, local recommendations, and even share interesting stories about the places you visit.

Using private shuttles not only offers comfort and convenience but also ensures a smooth and efficient travel experience. It allows you to relax and enjoy the scenic views without worrying about navigating unfamiliar roads or deciphering public transportation schedules.

Taxis:

Taxis are readily available in cities and towns throughout Nicaragua. They offer a convenient and flexible transportation option for both short-distance travel within a city and longer trips between different destinations.

When taking a taxi in Nicaragua, it is advisable to use licensed taxis or request them from your hotel or a reputable establishment. Licensed taxis usually display their identification and license numbers prominently, providing reassurance regarding their legitimacy and adherence to safety standards.

Before getting into a taxi, it is recommended to negotiate the fare with the driver or ensure that the meter is used.

Discussing the fare beforehand helps avoid any misunderstandings or potential overcharging. It's also a good idea to have small denominations of local currency, as taxi drivers may not always have change for larger bills.

Taxis in Nicaragua come in various forms, from regular sedans to smaller compact cars or even three-wheeled vehicles known as tuk-tuks. In some cities like Granada and León, you might come across colorful horse-drawn carriages known as "coches de caballo," which offer a unique and traditional mode of transportation.

Taxis provide the convenience of door-to-door service and are particularly useful when traveling with luggage or when exploring areas with limited public transportation options. They offer a more personalized experience compared to other modes of transportation, allowing you to interact with the local drivers and gain insights into the local culture and attractions.

In Nicaragua, there are several popular transportation system apps that can help make navigating the country more convenient. These apps provide access to ride-hailing services and help ensure a reliable and efficient transportation experience. Here are some popular transportation system apps in Nicaragua:

Uber: Uber is a widely recognized and utilized ride-hailing app that operates in various cities around the world, including several in Nicaragua. By using the Uber app, you can request a ride and track your driver's location in real-time. It provides a convenient and often cost-effective way to travel within cities like Managua and Granada.

DiDi: DiDi is another popular ride-hailing app that is available in Nicaragua. Similar to Uber, DiDi allows users to request rides and provides an estimated fare upfront. The app also offers features such as driver ratings, multiple payment options, and 24/7 customer support.

InDriver: InDriver is a ride-hailing app that operates in several cities across Nicaragua. What sets InDriver apart is its unique feature that allows passengers to propose their own fare to drivers, who can then either accept or negotiate the price. This system aims to provide more flexibility and affordability for users.

Cabify: Cabify is a transportation app that offers a range of services, including private cars, executive vehicles, and shared rides. It operates in select cities in Nicaragua, providing a reliable and comfortable transportation option for those who prefer a higher-end service.

These transportation apps can be downloaded from app stores and offer user-friendly interfaces that make it easy to request rides, track drivers, and make payments. It's important to note that availability and coverage may vary depending on the city or region within Nicaragua, so it's recommended to check the app for service availability in your desired location.

By using these transportation system apps, you can enjoy the convenience of on-demand rides, transparent pricing, and the ability to track your journey, making your travel experience in Nicaragua more efficient and hassle-free.

Whether you choose to fly domestically, embrace the local charm of public buses, enjoy the comfort of private shuttles, or opt for the convenience of taxis, Nicaragua provides a range of transportation options to suit every traveler's preferences and budget. Each mode of transport offers its own unique experiences, allowing you to make the most of your journey through this captivating Central American destination.

Accommodation Recommendations

Nicaragua offers a wide range of accommodation options to suit different budgets and preferences. Here are some recommendations to consider when choosing your accommodation:

Hotels and Resorts:

Nicaragua's hotel and resort scene caters to a wide range of travelers, from those seeking luxurious accommodations to budget-conscious adventurers. In popular tourist areas and cities, you'll find a diverse selection of options that offer comfortable stays and a variety of amenities.

Luxury Hotels and Resorts:

For travelers who prefer indulgence and top-notch services, Nicaragua boasts a collection of luxury hotels and resorts. These establishments provide an opulent experience, with elegant suites, breathtaking views, and world-class facilities. Many luxury properties are located in prime beachfront locations, offering direct access to pristine sands and crystal-clear waters. From private villas with plunge pools to spas offering rejuvenating treatments, these establishments spare no expense in pampering their guests. In addition, fine dining restaurants within the premises serve exquisite cuisine, often featuring locally sourced ingredients and international flavors.

Anecdote: Imagine waking up to the sound of waves crashing against the shore as you step onto the balcony of your luxurious suite overlooking the Pacific Ocean. The warm tropical breeze caresses your face as you indulge in a gourmet breakfast prepared by talented chefs. This is the experience awaiting you at one of Nicaragua's upscale resorts, where every detail is meticulously designed to provide an unforgettable stay.

Budget-Friendly Options:

Nicaragua also offers a variety of budget-friendly hotels and guesthouses, making it an accessible destination for travelers on a tighter budget. These accommodations are often located in popular tourist areas and cities, providing convenient access to attractions, restaurants, and transportation hubs. While they may not offer the same level of opulence as luxury resorts, they provide comfortable and clean rooms at affordable rates. Budget-friendly options may include amenities such as complimentary breakfast, Wi-Fi access, and helpful staff who can assist with travel arrangements and local recommendations.

Anecdote: During my backpacking adventure in Nicaragua, I discovered a charming budget hotel tucked away in the heart of a colonial city. The cozy guesthouse featured colorful murals, comfortable beds, and a communal courtyard where fellow travelers would gather to swap stories and plan their next adventures. Despite its modest price, the hotel provided a warm and welcoming atmosphere that made me feel right at home.

Boutique Hotels and Guesthouses:

For those seeking a more intimate and personalized experience, boutique hotels and guesthouses in Nicaragua are the perfect choice. These accommodations often feature unique architecture, local artwork, and stylish interiors that reflect the country's rich cultural heritage. Boutique hotels are typically smaller in size, allowing for more attentive service and a sense of exclusivity. Many of these establishments are family-owned and operated, creating a warm and inviting atmosphere where guests can interact with the owners and gain insights into the local culture.

Anecdote: As I stepped into the lobby of a boutique hotel nestled within a colonial town, I was immediately captivated by its charm. The restored colonial building exuded history and character, with each room decorated with handcrafted furniture and vibrant artwork. The owner greeted me personally, sharing stories about the town's heritage and recommending hidden gems that only a local would know. It was an authentic and enriching experience that left a lasting impression on my journey through Nicaragua.

Eco-Lodges:

Nicaragua's commitment to sustainable tourism is evident in its eco-lodges, which provide comfortable stays while minimizing the environmental impact. These lodges are often nestled in pristine natural settings, such as rainforests, cloud forests, or near volcanoes. Designed to blend harmoniously with their surroundings, eco-lodges offer a unique opportunity to immerse yourself in nature while practicing responsible travel. They employ eco-friendly practices, such as using renewable energy, recycling, and promoting conservation efforts. Guests can engage in eco-tours, nature hikes, birdwatching, and other outdoor activities, guided by knowledgeable staff who prioritize environmental education and preservation.

Anecdote: Tucked away in the heart of a tropical rainforest, I discovered an eco-lodge that seemed to be in perfect harmony with nature. The lodge's bungalows were built with sustainable materials, offering stunning views of the surrounding lush greenery. Solar panels provided electricity, and the water supply came from natural springs. Each morning, I woke up to the melodious symphony of birds and the rustling of leaves. The lodge's knowledgeable guides led me on captivating hikes through the rainforest, where I encountered vibrant wildlife and learned about the importance of preserving this precious ecosystem.

Hostels:

Hostels have long been a popular choice for budget-conscious travelers and backpackers exploring Nicaragua. They provide affordable accommodations, often in the form of dormitory-style rooms, where guests can meet like-minded individuals from around the world. Hostels are not just a place to sleep; they are vibrant social hubs with communal areas where travelers can relax, cook meals together, and share travel stories. Private rooms are also available in some hostels for those seeking more privacy while still enjoying the social atmosphere.

Anecdote: Staying at a hostel in Nicaragua opened up a world of new friendships and unforgettable experiences. In the common area, I met fellow travelers with diverse backgrounds, exchanging tales of our adventures and forming lifelong bonds. We embarked on group excursions to nearby waterfalls, explored local markets together, and even organized impromptu salsa dancing lessons. The hostel's friendly staff provided invaluable tips and recommendations, ensuring we made the most of our time in Nicaragua on a shoestring budget.

When it comes to finding and booking accommodation in Nicaragua, there are several popular apps and websites that can assist you in your search. Here are some widely used platforms:

Airbnb: Airbnb is a well-known online marketplace that connects travelers with hosts offering various accommodations, including apartments, houses, villas, and even unique stays like treehouses or beachfront bungalows. You can browse through listings, read reviews, and book directly through the app or website.

Booking.com: Booking.com is a widely used platform that offers a wide range of accommodation options, from hotels and resorts to guesthouses and hostels. The app provides user-friendly filters and search functions to help you find the perfect place based on your preferences and budget. It also offers free cancellation on many properties.

Expedia: Expedia is a comprehensive travel platform that allows you to search and book accommodations, flights, and rental cars. It provides a wide selection of hotels and resorts across Nicaragua, along with user reviews, photos, and detailed descriptions to assist in making an informed decision.

Hotels.com: Hotels.com specializes in hotel bookings and offers a vast selection of properties in Nicaragua. The app features a user-friendly interface, special deals, and a loyalty program that rewards you with a free night after booking a certain number of nights.

TripAdvisor: TripAdvisor is a popular platform that provides a wealth of information and user reviews on accommodations, attractions, and restaurants. It can be a valuable resource for researching and comparing different options in Nicaragua. TripAdvisor also allows you to book directly through their platform.

Agoda: Agoda is a leading online travel agency that specializes in Asia but also offers a wide range of accommodation options worldwide, including Nicaragua. The app features a user-friendly interface, special discounts, and a loyalty program for additional savings.

Hostelworld: If you're specifically looking for hostel accommodations, Hostelworld is a go-to platform. It offers an extensive selection of hostels in Nicaragua and allows you to read reviews, view photos, and book directly through the app or website.

These apps and websites provide convenient ways to search, compare, and book accommodations in Nicaragua. They often include filters based on location, price range, amenities, and guest ratings to help you find the perfect place that suits your preferences and travel needs.

Whether you prefer the lavishness of luxury hotels, the personalized touch of boutique accommodations, the eco-consciousness of eco-lodges, or the social atmosphere of hostels, Nicaragua offers a wide array of options to suit every traveler's preferences and budget. With these diverse choices, you can find the perfect accommodation to enhance your journey through this captivating Central American country.

Safety and Health Guidelines

Ensuring your safety and well-being is essential while traveling in Nicaragua. Here are some safety and health guidelines to keep in mind:

Personal Safety:

When traveling to any destination, including Nicaragua, it's essential to prioritize personal safety. By following some simple precautions, you can minimize potential risks and ensure a smooth and secure journey.

Be Mindful of Your Surroundings: Nicaragua is generally a safe country for tourists, but it's always wise to be aware of your surroundings. Avoid displaying signs of wealth, such as expensive jewelry or electronic devices, as it may attract unwanted attention. Keep a low profile and blend in with the local culture to minimize the risk of becoming a target for theft or scams.

Stay in Well-Lit Areas: Whether you're exploring city streets or walking back to your accommodation at night, prioritize well-lit areas. Stick to main roads and avoid dark, secluded alleyways or poorly lit areas that could pose safety risks. If possible, travel with a companion, especially during nighttime excursions.

Use Reputable Transportation Options: When it comes to transportation, it's important to choose reliable and reputable options. Opt for registered taxis from established companies, or use ride-hailing services like Uber if available in the area. Avoid getting into unmarked or unofficial taxis to minimize the risk of encountering fraudulent drivers.

Be Cautious When Exploring Unfamiliar Places: While Nicaragua has numerous beautiful and safe areas to explore, it's advisable to exercise caution when venturing into unfamiliar places, especially at night. Research the areas you plan to visit beforehand and seek local advice or guidance if needed. Stick to well-known tourist destinations and avoid remote or isolated areas unless accompanied by a knowledgeable guide.

Health Precautions:

To ensure a healthy and enjoyable trip to Nicaragua, it's crucial to take appropriate health precautions and consult with healthcare professionals before your departure.

Consult Your Healthcare Provider: Before traveling, schedule an appointment with your healthcare provider or a travel clinic to discuss any necessary vaccinations or medications. They will assess your health condition and provide guidance on specific vaccines recommended for Nicaragua. Routine vaccines, such as measles, mumps, rubella, and tetanus-diphtheria-pertussis, should be up to date.

Mosquito-Borne Diseases: Nicaragua is located in a region where mosquito-borne diseases like dengue fever, Zika virus, and chikungunya can occur. To protect yourself from mosquito bites, use insect repellents containing DEET, wear long sleeves and pants, and consider staying in accommodations with air conditioning or mosquito nets. It's also advisable to sleep under a mosquito net, especially in more rural areas or during peak mosquito activity times.

Food and Water Safety: To avoid foodborne illnesses, it's important to be mindful of what you eat and drink in Nicaragua. Stick to bottled water or purified water, and avoid consuming tap water, including ice cubes. When dining out, choose reputable establishments with good hygiene practices. Wash your hands frequently with soap and water, especially before eating or handling food. If soap and water are not available, use hand sanitizers with at least 60% alcohol content.

Street Food: Nicaraguan street food can be tempting, offering a wide variety of flavors and local delicacies. While street food can be delicious, exercise caution when choosing vendors. Look for stalls with high customer turnover and where food is prepared freshly in front of you. Make sure the food is cooked thoroughly and served hot to reduce the risk of foodborne illnesses.

Water Purification: If you prefer to use tap water for drinking, consider using a water purifier or portable water filtration system. These devices can effectively remove harmful bacteria and parasites, providing you with safe drinking water even from questionable sources.

By being vigilant about personal safety, taking necessary health precautions, and practicing food and water safety measures, you can minimize potential risks and enjoy a healthy and worry-free trip to Nicaragua. Remember that these guidelines are meant to serve as general advice, and it's always recommended to consult with healthcare professionals and stay updated on travel advisories before your departure.

Communication and Internet Access

Staying connected and having access to communication facilities can be helpful during your trip. Here's what you need to know about communication and internet access in Nicaragua:

SIM Cards:

When traveling to Nicaragua, having a local SIM card can greatly enhance your communication capabilities and save you money on roaming charges. Local SIM cards are widely available throughout the country, and you can easily purchase them at the airport, mobile carrier stores, or authorized resellers.

Before buying a local SIM card, it's important to ensure that your phone is unlocked. Locked phones are typically tied to a specific mobile service provider and can only be used with their SIM cards. Unlocking your phone allows you to use SIM cards from different carriers, giving you the flexibility to choose the best option for your needs.

Once you have a local SIM card, you will be assigned a Nicaraguan phone number. This local number will allow you to make and receive calls within Nicaragua at local rates, making it more affordable compared to international roaming charges. Having a local number also makes it easier for locals and fellow travelers to contact you during your stay.

One of the major advantages of getting a local SIM card is the access to affordable data plans. Nicaraguan mobile service providers offer various data packages that cater to different usage needs. Whether you want to stay connected through social media, navigate with online maps, or simply browse the internet, purchasing a data plan will ensure you have a reliable and cost-effective internet connection.

Wi-Fi Availability:

While having a local SIM card provides you with mobile data, it's worth noting that Wi-Fi is readily available in many places across Nicaragua. Most hotels, resorts, cafes, and restaurants in popular tourist areas offer free Wi-Fi access to their guests. This allows you to connect your devices to the internet without using your mobile data.

However, it's important to keep in mind that the quality and speed of Wi-Fi connections can vary, especially in more remote or rural areas. In some cases, the Wi-Fi signal may be weaker or less reliable, which can affect the browsing speed and overall internet experience. It's a good idea to manage your expectations and have alternative options, such as a local SIM card, in case you encounter issues with Wi-Fi availability or performance.

Internet Cafes:

If you don't have a device or need to access the internet for a longer period of time, internet cafes are a convenient option. Major cities and towns in Nicaragua have internet cafes where you can use their computer terminals for a small fee. These cafes provide a comfortable environment with internet access, allowing you to browse the web, check emails, or even print documents if needed.

Internet cafes can be particularly helpful if you're traveling without a laptop or if you need to complete tasks that require more extensive computer use. Additionally, the staff at these cafes are usually knowledgeable about local attractions and services, so they can provide you with valuable information and recommendations during your visit.

Communication Apps:

Utilizing messaging and calling apps can be a cost-effective way to stay connected with your friends and family back home while in Nicaragua. Apps like WhatsApp, Skype, and Viber use internet connectivity instead of traditional phone networks, allowing you to send messages, make voice or video calls, and even share multimedia files.

Using communication apps is especially advantageous if you have access to Wi-Fi or a reliable data connection through a local SIM card. It's important to note that these apps consume data, so make sure you monitor your usage and consider purchasing a suitable data plan or connecting to Wi-Fi when available to avoid unexpected charges.

Anecdote:

John, an avid traveler, arrived in Nicaragua with his unlocked smartphone and was eager to get a local SIM card. He headed to a mobile carrier store near his hotel in Managua and purchased a SIM card with a data plan that suited his needs. Within minutes, his phone was activated with a Nicaraguan phone number, and he was ready to explore the country.

Throughout his journey, John found that having a local SIM card made a significant difference in his travel experience. He could easily navigate using online maps, search for recommendations on local attractions and restaurants, and share his adventures with friends on social media without worrying about excessive roaming charges.

While visiting Granada, John realized that the Wi-Fi at his hotel was intermittent, making it challenging to stay connected. However, he discovered that most cafes and restaurants in the city offered free Wi-Fi, allowing him to enjoy a cup of Nicaraguan coffee while catching up on emails and planning his next activities.

During his time in León, John needed to print out some important documents for an upcoming business meeting. Fortunately, he found a cozy internet cafe in the city center that provided computer terminals and printing services. The friendly staff even helped him find the nearest post office to send the documents securely.

To keep in touch with his family back home, John relied on messaging and calling apps. He used WhatsApp to send updates, photos, and voice messages, allowing his loved ones to stay connected with his Nicaraguan adventure in real-time. He also made video calls through Skype to share the stunning views of volcanoes and the vibrant culture he encountered along the way.

Before leaving Nicaragua, John ensured that he had settled any outstanding payments for his local SIM card and data plan. He was glad he had checked with his mobile service provider before his trip to understand the international roaming charges and data plans they offered. By being prepared, he avoided any surprises on his phone bill and could reminisce about his unforgettable journey through Nicaragua without any worries.

Remember to check with your mobile service provider regarding international roaming charges and data plans before using your phone in Nicaragua. Being informed about your options and having the right tools for communication will enhance your travel experience and ensure you stay connected throughout your Nicaraguan adventure.

By keeping these practical travel tips in mind, you'll be well-prepared to navigate transportation options, find suitable accommodations, ensure your safety and health, and stay connected during your adventure in Nicaragua.

Making a Difference: Sustainable Travel

Responsible Tourism in Nicaragua

Responsible tourism is a growing movement that recognizes the importance of minimizing the negative impacts of tourism on the environment, culture, and communities. Nicaragua, with its diverse ecosystems, stunning landscapes, and rich cultural heritage, presents a myriad of opportunities for responsible tourism. By adopting responsible practices, travelers can actively contribute to the preservation of Nicaragua's natural beauty and support the well-being of local communities.

One crucial aspect of responsible tourism in Nicaragua is respecting the environment. The country is home to an array of delicate ecosystems, including rainforests, coastal areas, and volcanic landscapes. To minimize your ecological footprint, it is essential to follow sustainable practices during your visit. Conserving water by taking shorter showers and reusing towels, for example, can significantly reduce water consumption. Additionally, being mindful of waste management and recycling wherever possible helps to mitigate the impact on local landfills and natural habitats.

One of the easiest ways to be environmentally conscious while traveling in Nicaragua is to avoid single-use plastics. Plastic waste is a global issue, and Nicaragua is no exception. By carrying a reusable water bottle and shopping bag, you can minimize the use of disposable plastic bottles and bags, thereby reducing plastic pollution. Many establishments, especially in popular tourist areas, are making efforts to offer alternatives to single-use plastics, such as refill stations for water bottles and biodegradable packaging.

Another way to engage in responsible tourism is by choosing eco-friendly accommodations. Nicaragua offers a range of environmentally conscious lodging options that prioritize energy efficiency, waste management, and sustainable practices. These establishments often employ renewable energy sources, such as solar panels, and implement recycling programs. By staying in eco-lodges or hotels with sustainable certifications, you can directly support businesses that are committed to reducing their environmental impact.

One notable example of eco-friendly accommodations in Nicaragua is Jicaro Island Ecolodge, located on a private island in Lake Nicaragua. This unique lodge runs entirely on solar power, utilizes rainwater harvesting systems, and implements various conservation initiatives. Guests can enjoy a luxurious and comfortable stay while knowing that their presence is contributing to the preservation of the surrounding natural environment.

In addition to environmental responsibility, responsible tourism in Nicaragua also focuses on supporting and respecting local communities. Nicaragua is a country with a vibrant cultural heritage and a strong sense of community. Engaging with local traditions, customs, and businesses is an enriching way to experience the authentic Nicaraguan way of life while promoting sustainable tourism.

One way to support local communities is through conscious spending. By purchasing locally made products and souvenirs, travelers contribute to the local economy and help sustain traditional crafts and artisanal skills. For instance, in the city of Masaya, renowned for its handicrafts, visitors can explore the Masaya Artisan Market, where local artisans showcase their handcrafted ceramics, textiles, and artwork. By buying directly from these artisans, travelers not only acquire unique and meaningful souvenirs but also support the preservation of Nicaragua's cultural heritage.

Volunteering and engaging in community initiatives provide another avenue for responsible tourism in Nicaragua. Many organizations and projects in the country focus on sustainable development, education, healthcare, and conservation efforts. By dedicating your time and skills to these initiatives, you can make a tangible difference in the lives of Nicaraguans and actively contribute to the country's long-term growth.

For example, the FNE International (Fundación Nica en Acción) is a non-profit organization that offers volunteer opportunities in Nicaragua. They collaborate with local communities to implement projects related to education, healthcare, and infrastructure development. Volunteers can contribute their expertise in fields such as teaching English, construction, healthcare assistance, or community development, thereby fostering positive change in the lives of Nicaraguan individuals and communities.

Furthermore, engaging in eco-tours and activities that promote sustainable practices and conservation efforts is another way to participate in responsible tourism. These activities often provide educational experiences that increase awareness about the importance of preserving Nicaragua's natural ecosystems and cultural heritage.

Anecdotal evidence from responsible travelers who have visited Nicaragua further emphasizes the impact of responsible tourism on local communities and the environment. For instance, Lisa, a traveler from the United States, recalls her experience volunteering at a local school in Granada, Nicaragua. Through her involvement, she not only contributed to the education of local children but also forged meaningful connections with the community. Lisa learned about the challenges faced by Nicaraguan schools and was inspired to initiate fundraising efforts upon her return home, which successfully raised funds for educational supplies and infrastructure improvements.

In another instance, Mark, an avid hiker and nature enthusiast, shares his experience of participating in an eco-tour to the Mombacho Volcano Nature Reserve. During the tour, he learned about the reserve's conservation initiatives and the importance of protecting the cloud forest ecosystem. Mark was impressed by the knowledgeable local guides who emphasized the significance of sustainable tourism practices and how the revenue generated from tourism directly contributes to the preservation of the reserve and supports the livelihoods of local communities.

Community Initiatives and Volunteering Opportunities

Nicaragua is a country that truly values community and recognizes the importance of supporting its local populations. From sustainable development to education, healthcare, and conservation, numerous organizations and projects in Nicaragua are dedicated to uplifting communities and fostering long-term growth. By volunteering your time and skills, you have the opportunity to make a positive impact on the lives of Nicaraguans and contribute to the country's progress.

One of the popular avenues for volunteering in Nicaragua is teaching English. English language skills open doors to better opportunities for locals, especially in the tourism industry. Many schools and organizations across the country welcome volunteers to assist in English language programs. By sharing your language proficiency and teaching methods, you can empower Nicaraguans with valuable skills that enhance their employability and broaden their horizons.

In addition to education, volunteering in community development projects is another meaningful way to contribute. These projects focus on improving infrastructure, access to clean water, and overall quality of life in local communities. You may have the opportunity to collaborate with local residents, lending a helping hand in construction, renovation, or community beautification projects. Through these initiatives, you will witness firsthand the transformative power of collective effort and the positive changes that can occur when communities unite for a common goal.

Nicaragua is also known for its vibrant artisanal traditions. Volunteering with local artisans provides a unique opportunity to learn about traditional craftsmanship while supporting sustainable livelihoods. Whether it's working with skilled potters, weavers, or woodworkers, you can contribute to the preservation of these age-old techniques and help artisans thrive in an increasingly globalized world. By participating in workshops, assisting with marketing initiatives, or organizing exhibitions, you can directly support the local artisans and their communities.

Environmental conservation is another crucial area where volunteers can make a significant impact in Nicaragua. With its rich biodiversity and diverse ecosystems, the country offers ample opportunities to contribute to conservation efforts. Organizations and initiatives focus on reforestation, wildlife protection, and sustainable agriculture practices. Through hands-on participation in activities such as tree planting, habitat restoration, or wildlife monitoring, you can actively contribute to the preservation of Nicaragua's natural wonders for future generations to enjoy.

One inspiring example of a volunteer-driven conservation project in Nicaragua is the sea turtle conservation programs along the country's Pacific and Caribbean coasts. These programs aim to protect endangered sea turtle species, such as the Olive Ridley, Leatherback, and Hawksbill turtles. Volunteers participate in activities such as night patrols to monitor nesting behavior, protecting nests from poachers or predators, and releasing hatchlings into the ocean. By being part of these programs, volunteers directly contribute to the conservation of these magnificent creatures and raise awareness about the importance of marine biodiversity.

Volunteering in Nicaragua offers much more than just lending a helping hand. It allows you to immerse yourself in the country's vibrant culture, forge meaningful connections with locals, and gain a deeper understanding of the challenges and triumphs faced by Nicaraguans. You'll have the chance to exchange stories, share laughter, and create lasting memories with the people you meet. The friendships and connections formed during your volunteer experience will leave an indelible mark on both you and the local community.

Moreover, the impact of volunteering extends beyond the immediate benefits. By supporting sustainable development, education, healthcare, and conservation efforts, volunteers contribute to the long-term growth and well-being of

Nicaragua. The skills and knowledge transferred during your time as a volunteer can continue to empower individuals and communities, creating a ripple effect that extends far beyond your stay.

It's important to research and choose reputable volunteer organizations or projects that align with your interests and values. Consider factors such as the organization's track record, transparency, and community involvement. Engage in open communication with the organization to understand their objectives and how your skills can be effectively utilized. This way, you can ensure that your volunteer experience in Nicaragua is meaningful, ethical, and truly contributes to the betterment of the local community.

Eco-friendly Practices for Travelers

Traveling sustainably involves making conscious choices that minimize harm to the environment and local communities. Here are some eco-friendly practices to consider when exploring Nicaragua:

Use reusable water bottles and shopping bags to reduce plastic waste.

One of the simplest and most effective ways to reduce plastic waste while traveling in Nicaragua is to bring and use reusable water bottles and shopping bags. Nicaragua, like many other destinations, faces challenges with plastic pollution, particularly in coastal areas and natural reserves. By utilizing reusable bottles and bags, travelers can significantly reduce their consumption of single-use plastics and contribute to a cleaner and more sustainable environment.

When exploring cities, towns, or even remote areas, carrying a reusable water bottle is essential. Nicaragua's tap water is generally safe to drink in urban areas, so refilling your bottle from local water sources can save you from purchasing bottled water and prevent countless plastic bottles from ending up in landfills or polluting the environment. Additionally, investing in a high-quality reusable water bottle ensures durability throughout your trip, allowing you to stay hydrated while minimizing plastic waste.

Similarly, having reusable shopping bags on hand is invaluable when visiting local markets, grocery stores, or souvenir shops. Nicaraguan markets are vibrant and filled with fresh produce, local crafts, and unique products. By bringing your own bag, you can avoid accepting single-use plastic bags offered by vendors and contribute to reducing plastic waste. Moreover, using a reusable bag often sparks conversations with locals and fellow travelers, providing an opportunity to raise awareness about sustainable practices and the importance of reducing plastic consumption.

Opt for public transportation or eco-friendly transportation options, such as biking or walking, whenever possible.

Nicaragua offers various transportation options for travelers, and consciously choosing eco-friendly alternatives can significantly reduce your carbon footprint and contribute to sustainable tourism. When navigating within cities or towns, consider using public transportation systems like buses or shared taxis. Not only is public transportation generally more affordable, but it also helps decrease traffic congestion and air pollution.

For shorter distances, embrace the beauty of Nicaragua by opting for environmentally friendly transportation modes such as biking or walking. Many cities and towns have bike rental services or guided bike tours available, allowing you to explore at your own pace while enjoying the fresh air and scenic routes. Additionally, walking provides an immersive experience, enabling you to discover hidden gems, interact with locals, and fully appreciate the beauty of your surroundings.

Respect wildlife and natural habitats by observing animals from a distance and refraining from disturbing their natural behavior.

Nicaragua is blessed with incredible biodiversity, encompassing lush rainforests, pristine beaches, and diverse ecosystems. When encountering wildlife in their natural habitats, it is crucial to observe them respectfully and responsibly. Respecting wildlife not only ensures their well-being but also allows future generations to enjoy the same encounters.

Whether it's encountering monkeys swinging through the treetops, spotting exotic birds, or glimpsing sea turtles nesting on the beaches, maintaining a safe distance is essential. Approaching too closely or attempting to touch or feed wild animals can cause stress, disrupt their natural behavior, and even endanger both the animals and yourself. Instead, use binoculars or a zoom lens to observe them from a distance, allowing them to carry on with their daily activities undisturbed.

Support local businesses and artisans by purchasing locally made products and souvenirs.

One of the most rewarding aspects of traveling in Nicaragua is the opportunity to support local communities and artisans. By purchasing locally made products and souvenirs, you directly contribute to the local economy, empower local artisans, and help preserve traditional crafts and cultural heritage.

Nicaragua is known for its vibrant arts and crafts scene, with each region showcasing its unique creations. Whether it's intricately woven textiles, handcrafted ceramics, wooden carvings, or indigenous artwork, there is a wide array of authentic products to choose from. Seek out local markets, cooperative stores, or artisan workshops to find these treasures. Engaging with artisans and learning about their techniques and cultural significance adds depth and meaning to your purchases.

Conserve energy by turning off lights and air conditioning when not in use and using energy-efficient accommodations.

Conserving energy is an essential part of sustainable travel. By adopting simple habits and choosing energy-efficient accommodations, you can minimize your environmental impact while enjoying a comfortable stay in Nicaragua.

When staying in hotels or accommodations, be mindful of your energy usage. Turn off lights, air conditioning, and other appliances when not in use or when leaving your room. Simple actions like unplugging chargers and electronics that are not in use can also help reduce unnecessary energy consumption. By being conscious of your energy usage, you can contribute to lowering greenhouse gas emissions and conserving valuable resources.

Furthermore, consider staying in accommodations that prioritize energy efficiency and sustainable practices. Many eco-lodges and hotels in Nicaragua employ renewable energy sources, such as solar power, and implement water-saving measures. These establishments often blend harmoniously with the natural surroundings, allowing you to experience the beauty of Nicaragua while minimizing your ecological footprint.

Participate in eco-tours and activities that promote sustainable practices and conservation efforts.

Engaging in eco-tours and activities aligned with sustainable practices and conservation efforts is an excellent way to support local initiatives and learn more about Nicaragua's unique ecosystems. These experiences allow you to connect with nature, gain insight into conservation efforts, and contribute directly to the preservation of Nicaragua's natural heritage.

In Nicaragua, there are eco-tours available in various regions, offering opportunities such as guided hikes in national parks, wildlife spotting excursions, birdwatching tours, and sustainable fishing experiences. These activities are usually led by knowledgeable guides who provide valuable information about the environment, wildlife, and ongoing conservation projects.

By participating in eco-tours, you contribute financially to the protection of natural areas, the employment of local guides, and the educational programs conducted by conservation organizations. Furthermore, these experiences often emphasize the importance of responsible and sustainable practices, allowing you to deepen your understanding of the local ecosystem and its conservation challenges.

By adopting these eco-friendly practices, you can enjoy your trip to Nicaragua while minimizing your ecological impact and supporting sustainable tourism initiatives.

Conclusion

In concluding this Nicaragua Travel Guide, it is important to reflect on the incredible experiences and memories you will have gathered during your journey through this Central American jewel. Nicaragua offers a unique blend of natural wonders, rich history, vibrant culture, and thrilling adventures that leave a lasting impression on every traveler.

As you bid farewell to Nicaragua, take a moment to appreciate the beauty and diversity of this remarkable country. Whether you found yourself exploring the rainforests, lounging on pristine beaches, or climbing volcanoes, each moment was an opportunity for personal growth and discovery.

Leaving Nicaragua with unforgettable memories is inevitable. The sights, sounds, and flavors of this captivating nation will linger in your mind long after you return home. From the colonial architecture of Granada to the revolutionary history of León, you have witnessed the layers of Nicaragua's past and its impact on the present.

As you prepare to depart, consider the lessons you have learned and the insights gained from your interactions with the local communities. Nicaragua's warm and welcoming people have undoubtedly left a mark on your heart. Embrace the memories and the connections you have made, and carry them with you as you continue your journey in life.

Before you go, here are some last words of advice. First and foremost, always be respectful of the local customs and traditions. Nicaraguans take pride in their culture, and by embracing it, you will forge deeper connections and gain a more authentic experience.

Additionally, consider the impact of your travel choices on the environment and local communities. Sustainable and responsible tourism practices can help preserve the natural beauty of Nicaragua and support the livelihoods of its residents. Leave no trace, support local businesses, and contribute positively to the destinations you visit.

Lastly, keep an open mind and be willing to step out of your comfort zone. Nicaragua is a land of surprises, and some of the most memorable moments come from unexpected encounters and spontaneous adventures. Embrace the spirit of adventure and allow yourself to be fully present in each moment.

Leaving Nicaragua doesn't mean saying goodbye forever. It means carrying a piece of Nicaragua within you, sharing your experiences with others, and perhaps even returning one day to continue your exploration of this enchanting country. May your memories of Nicaragua always bring a smile to your face and a yearning to embark on new adventures wherever life takes you.

Printed in Great Britain
by Amazon

32801698R00096